D. J. Bannell Sawyer

Sawyer's manual of book-keeping

Theoretical and practical. Second Edition

D. J. Bannell Sawyer

Sawyer's manual of book-keeping
Theoretical and practical. Second Edition

ISBN/EAN: 9783744785730

Printed in Europe, USA, Canada, Australia, Japan

Cover: Foto ©Lupo / pixelio.de

More available books at **www.hansebooks.com**

SAWYER'S
MANUAL OF BOOK-KEEPING

THEORETICAL AND PRACTICAL.

— FOR —

THE USE OF STUDENTS

— IN —

Business Colleges, Commercial Departments, High Schools and Academies,

— ALSO —

Private Students without the aid of a Teacher.

— BY —

D. J. BANNELL SAWYER,

Author of "Text Book of Business Writing;" "Original System of Penmanship;" "Studies for Real Life;" "Universal Shorthand," Etc.

SECOND EDITION.

COPYRIGHTED.

OTTAWA, ONT:
PUBLISHED BY THE COLLEGE,
1889.

PREFACE.

SECOND EDITION.

LITTLE, by way of preface to a book, is needed now-a-days. The reader can generally write a truer estimate of a book than its author. However, the author believes this book to be practical and useful, and if others find it so, he will be amply repaid for the burden of its production. It is not yet what he wishes it to be, and yet, there is enough of it to be of great service to anyone desiring a practical knowledge of accounts. The first 96 pages should be thoroughly understood before attempting to write up the sets.

We hereby gratefully acknowledge the many favors received at the hands of the public during the past fifteen years of authorship, and especially for a very liberal patronage during the year just closing.

In the hope that this edition may be of still greater use to the young people of Canada than the former one, I remain,

Very respectfully,

BANNELL SAWYER.

OTTAWA, 20 November, 1889.

COMMERCIAL ABBREVIATIONS.
FREQUENTLY USED IN ACCOUNTING, &c.

1 Acct.—Account.
2 Acct'nt.—Accountant.
3 Amt.—Amount.
4 Ans.—Answer.
5 Agrmnt.—Agreement.
6 Apr—April.
7 Aug.—August.
8 Bbls. Barrels.
9 Bk.—Book.
10 Bot.—Bought.
11 Brot.—Brought

12 Blk—Black.
13 B. Ex.—Bill of Exchange.
14 B. En.—Bill of Entry.
15 B. L —Bill of Lading.
16 Bal.—Balance.
17 B. P. B.—Bank Pass Book.
18 B. B.—Bill Book.
19 B. S. B.—Balance Sheet Book.
20 B. Rec.—Bills Receivable.
21 B. Pay.—Bills Payable.
22 Bd. Pay.—Bond Payable.

COMMERCIAL ABBREVIATIONS—(*Continued*).

23 Ck.—Check.
24 Ck. B—Check Book.
25 Cap.—Capital.
26 Certf.—Certificate.
27 C. B.—Cash Book.
28 C of D.—Certificate of Deposit.
29 C. O. D.—Collect on Delivery.
30 Co —Company.
31 Consgt. B.—Consignment Book.
32 Com —Commission.
33 Consgt.—Consignment.
34 Cwt.—Hundred Weight.
35 Chgd.—Charged.
36 Cr.—Creditor.
37 Cts.—Cents.
38 D.—Pence.
39 Dec.—December.
40 Dr.—Debtor.
41 Doz.—Dozen.
42 D. B.—Day Book.
43 Ds.—Days.
44 Dft,—Drafts.
45 Dis.—Discount.
46 Do—Ditto or The Same.
47 Du. B.—Due Bill. [ex'td]
48 E & O. E.—Errors and Omissions
49 Ea.—Each.
50 Exch —Exchange.
51 Exp.—Express.
52 Entd.—Entered.
53 E —Example.
54 Feb.—February.
55 F. O. B. - Free on Board.
56 Fol —Folio.
57 For. Foreign.
58 Frt.—Freight.
59 Gal.—Gallon.
60 Gen. L.—General Ledger.
61 Hhd.—Hogshead.
62 I. B,—Invoice Book.
63 Hun —Hundred.
64 i. e.—That is.
65 Inst.—Instant.
66 Int. Interest.
67 Inv.—Invoice.
68 Invty.—Inventory.
69 J.—Journal.
70 J. F—Journal Folio.
71 Jan.—January.
72 Lbs—Pounds.
73 L. B.——Letter Book.
74 L. F—Ledger Folio.
75 L. & G.—Loss and Gain.
76 M.—Thousand.
77 Mar.—March.
78 Memo.—Memorandum.

79 Mfg.—Manufacturing.
80 Mos —Months.
81 N. B.—Note well.
82 No.—Number.
83 Nov.—November.
84 O B—Order Book.
85 O. I. B—Outward I. B.—
86 Oz—Ounce.
87 P.—Page.
88 PP.—Pages
89 Pcs.—Pieces.
90 Pd —Paid.
91 P. C. B—Petty C. B.
92 Per.—By.
93 P. B.—Pass B.
94 P. O —Post Office.
95 Pol.—Policy.
96 Pkg.—Package.
97 Prem.—Premium.
98 Pt. Pint.
99 Prox.—Proximo—next month.
100 Qt.—Quart.
101 Qr.—Quarter.
102 Recd —Received.
103 Recpt—Receipt.
104 Reg.—Regular or Register.
105 Ro —Right hand folio.
106 R. B.—Receipt Book.
107 R. R.—Railroad.
108 Ry.—Railway.
109 Sat.—Saturday.
110 Sec.—Secretary.
111 S B.—Sales Book.
112 Shipt —Shipment.
113 Sq.—Square.
114 St.—Street.
115 Stg.—Sterling.
116 Sunds.—Sundries.
117 T. B—Trial Balance.
118 Thurs.—Thursday.
119 Ult.—Ultimo—last month.
120 Viz —namely.
121 W B,—Way Bill.
122 Wed.—Wednesday.
123 Wt.—Weight.
124 Yds.—Yards.
125 Yr.—Year.
126 @—at.
127 ✓ —check mark.
128 %—per cent.
129 #—Number.
130 $—Dollars.
131 £—Pounds, 4 dollars.
132 Vs.—Versus—against.
133 =—Sign of Equality.
134 F. O. C.—Free on Cars.

HOME WORK.

The student on beginning his course should set to work to master all home work indicated in this Manual.

By faithful plodding at home during evenings—studying up "final exams," posting work gone over during the day, etc., etc.,—the industrious student may greatly shorten his term of attendance at the College. Those who are anxious to shorten their stay, can nearly double, by home study, the work of the term. To faithful plodders we attach the "WHITE SEAL" to their Diploma, upon graduation, in addition to the "Scarlet Seal" attached to all Diplomas issued. *An examination* will be given on this work when a student seeks *honors*.

1. Student began business with capital of $5000. At the close of the year his books exhibit the following facts :

Cash received $15,000 ; Cash paid out $12,000 ; A.B's a/c Dr. $1500 ; Cr $2600 ; B. C. ; Dr. $2400., Cr. $1200 ; C. D's Dr. $795 ; Cr $500; D.E's Dr. $830.75 ; Cr. $530.

Inventory of Mdse on hand $3550 ; Student owes E. H. $1100. Required, the net capital at closing, and the net gain during business.

2. Jones and Smith have begun business with the following resources : Cash $2000 ; Promissory Notes $1250 ; Mdse $5320 ; Real Estate $9,500 : Personal accounts (balances) due to firm $1,500. At the close of the year their resources and liabilities are as follows: Cash, on hand $1250 ; Cash in Bank of Ottawa $2000. Promissory Notes $4800 ; Merchandise, $5750 ; Real Estate $12,500. Due to firm on Personal Accounts $6,500. Due by firm on their notes issued and drafts accepted $875. Amount due by firm to persons on a/c $1675.

Required, the net capital at commencing ; at closing ; and net gain.

HOME WORK TESTS.

General

1.—What is book-keeping ?
2.—How many leading methods are there ?
3.—What are the main books used ?
4.—What does each contain ?
5.—What is an account ?

6.—What other books are used in account keeping?
7.—Into what two classes may we arrange accounts?
8.—Give three rules for debiting and three for crediting?
9.—What is generally included under the title Expense?
10.—What is generally included under the titles Cash, Mdse., B Rec., B. Pay., Interest and Discount.

Terms.

1.—Explain what is meant by Stock Account, Private Account, Cash Account, Balance Account, Representative Account, Personal Account, Expense Account, Loss and Gain Account.
2.—Define Draft, Note, Receipt, Bills of Exchange, Resource, Liability, Loss, Gain, Consignee, Consignor, Cheque, Proceeds of Note.
3.—Trial Balance; Balance Sheet, Posting, Blank Credit, Invoice, Drawback, Bill Book, Consignment, Shipment.
4.—What is an Acceptance, Due Bill, Lease, Manifest, Bill of Lading, Order, Mortgage, Bond?
5.—When are Exchange, Premium, Collection, Storage and Commission Accounts opened.

Skill.

1.—Upon closing Mdse. account, how do you ascertain the Gain or Loss?
2.—When do we debit, and when credit, the following accounts :— Cash, Mdse., Bills Payable, Loss and Gain, Interest, Stock, Private, J. Jones?
3.—In making out your statements preparatory to closing the Ledger, where do you place the following items:—Mdse. on Hand, Balance of Real Estate, Coal for use of Store, Money in Bank, Interest receivable, Balance of Interest.
4.—Mark off four columns with the following headings :—Resource, Liability, Loss, Gain, and put the following accounts into the column to which it belongs:—Cash, Mdse., Bank, Bank Stock, Real Estate, Expense, Rent, Freight, Shipment, Consignment, J. Jones, S. Evans.
5.—How far is the Trial Balance a test of correct work?

To Journalize.

1.—Sold Mdse. for cash $150

2.—Sold Mdse. to J. Jones for cash, $750.
3.—Sold S. Evans on ac., Mdse., invoiced at $500.
4.—Bot Mdse. for cash $200.
5.—Bot of J. Jones, Mdse., for cash, $135.
6.—Bot of S. Evans on ac., Mdse., $225.
7.—Bot Mdse. for note $50.
8.—Bot Mdse of R. Wood, for my note at 10 days, $35.
9.—Sold Mdse. to S. Smith, for check on Ontario Bank, $25.
10.—Bot Mdse. of J. Swift, for check on Ontario Bank, $20.
11.—S. Woods deposited cash in Bank of Toronto, $200.
12.—S. Woods withdraws from B. of T. $100. (Write check.)
13.—S. Swift gives J. Jones his note, at 3 months from to-day, for $521. (Write note.)
14.—Geo. A. Cox, of Peterborough, draws, to-day, a sight draft for $57 on Geo. Wilson & Sons, Port Hope. (Write draft.)
15.—Bot of J. W. Flavelle, 200 bbls. of flour @ $6 per bbl. Gave $500 in cash, my note for $300 ; balance to remain on ac.
16.—Sold J. W. Flavelle 1200 yds. broad-cloth @ $2.50. Rec'd in payment, cash $500, his note for $300 ; balance paid by an order on Hawley Bros.
17.—Wm. Dunn and I exchange notes, $250.
18.—Lost a $10 bill.
19.—$10 bill found and returned by Willie Snyder, who receives for his honesty $1.25.
20.—Discount your own note at College Bank for $700 @ 3 mos. rate 7 %.

FOR DRILLS.

1. TRANSACTION.—Peterborough, March 1st, 1889. You borrow $30 from E. B. Stone, and give him your note for $35, at 30 days in payment.
   1. Write this note making it payable to order. 2. When will it be due. 3. What per cent. of amount borrowed does the interest equal
2. TRANSACTION.—St. Thomas, March 5th, 1889. E. B. Stone has your note discounted at Bank of Toronto at 7%
   1. Write endorsement. 2. How much cash does he receive.
3. TRANSACTION.—St. Thomas, March .th, 1889. Sold J. B. Clarris, Esq., 20 yds. Silk at $1.50 ; 20 yds. S. Velvet at $2.50 ; 25

yds. B. Ribbon at 20c. ; 42 yds Edging at 16c. Received in payment his check on Bank of Toronto, for amount of bill. 1. Write out the bill. 2. Receipt it. 3. Write out check payable to order. 4. Indorse check making it payable to E. B. Snelgrove's order.

4. TRANSACTION.—Toronto, April 1st, 1889. John Macdonald draws a draft at 60 days sight on S. H. Blake, Toronto, for the balance of his account. The draft is in favor of Russel, Forbes & Co., Ottawa.

1. Write the draft. 2. Accept it for S. H. Blake, date April 2nd. 3. Discount at B. of T, 7 %. 4. Indorse it for Russel, Forbes & Co. 5. How much should R., F. & Co. receive.

5. TRANSACTION.—John Macdonald, of Toronto, owes Russel, Forbes & Co., Ottawa, $250, and Russel, Forbes & Co. owe James McLaren, of same place, $210. R. F. & Co. draw at 30 days sight on J. Macdonald in favor of McLaren for $210, and at sight in their own favor, for balance.

1. Write these drafts each dated May 1st, 1890. 2. Accept them for J. M. 3. Who will present the draft, R. F. & Co's. representative or McLaren's representative? 4. Write R. F. & Co's. advice to J. M. 5. Write their letter to McLaren.

6. TRANSACTION.—James Stevenson, Peterborough, encloses $150, Cash, to Williams & Co., Toronto; also a 90 day note dated April 1st, 1889, for $100, asking premission to close his running account by a 60 day note.

1. Write Stevenson's letter. 2. Write the 90 day note. 3. When is it due. 4. Write Williams & Co's favorable reply. 5. Endorse note for Williams & Co., payable to order of Jas. Kendry. 6. Find interest on this note at 6 %. 7. Find discount at 7 %.

RENEWING NOTES.

(a) Suppose your note matures at the Bank of Ottawa for $100 and you cannot pay it, if it be renewed and interest added, your entry would be as below. See (*a*).

The firm renewing the note need not make an entry, but should indicate in the B.B. Remarks' column the old note as retired by the renewal, and then enter the renewal in the bill book as received.

(b) If the firm endorsing the note has had it discounted and they

retire it by check, they would make an entry as follows, at the same time drawing on you for face of old note plus the charges, see (b):

(a)	Bills Pay Dr.	$100.		(b)	Bills Rec. Dr.	$105.	
	Int. "	5.			To Bills Rec...		100.
	To B. Pay...	$105.			" Interest		5.

If the above transactions were put through the personal account they would stand as follows:

(a)	B. Pay Dr.......	$100.		and			
	Int. "	5.		(a)	Holder of N. Dr..,	$105.	
	To Holder of Note	$105.			To B. Pay......		$105.

(b)	Student Dr.	$105.		and			
	To Bank......	$100.		(b)	B. Rec. Dr......	$105.	
	" Interest....	5.			To Student		$105.

Suppose you had renewed one-half and paid cash one-half, by first method, entries would be as follows:

(a)	Bills Pay Dr......	$100.		(b)	Bills Rec. Dr......	$52.50	
	Interest "	2.50			Cash "	50.	
	To Cash.	50.			To B. Rec.... .		100.
	" Bills Pay....	52.50			" Interest		2.50

NOTE.—If you had paid the charges on renewal in cash it would not have changed the *form* of this entry, but would simply swell the cash item by amount of charges.

PROMISSORY NOTES.

7. Find (1 When does the paper mature? (2) Where and to whom is it payable? (3) From what date does it draw interest? (5) What is the rate? (6) Which papers are endorsed in blank? (7) In full? (8) Without recourse? (9) Restrictively? (10) How are payments on notes recorded? (11) Compute and verify the interest on all interest-bearing papers? (12) What are days of grace good for?

FACE OF NOTE.	Payments Endorsed on BACK OF NOTE.
$1000. Peterboro', Ont., Jan. 4, 1889.	March 4th, 1889.
	Received on within note, Two Hundred and Fifty Dollars.
Three years after date, I promise to pay to the order of GEORGE A. COX, One Thousand Dollars, value received, with interest at 6 per cent. per annum.	December 5th, 1890.
	Received on within note, One Hundred and Ten Dollars.
	March 7th, 1891.
No. 1. WILLIAM WILLIAM.	Received on within note, Two Hundred and Twenty Dollars.

FACE OF NOTE.	Transfer and Payment. Endorsements on BACK OF NOTE
$2000. Peterboro', Ont., Jan. 4, 1889. Three years after date, for value received, I promise to pay to the order of MANN & Co., Two Thousand Dollars, with interest at 7 per cent, per annum, payable half-yearly. No. 2. JOHN FENTON.	Received July 4th, 1889, Seventy Dollars, Interest on within note in full to date. J. MANN & Co. Pay to W. Williams only, S. EVANS. January 4th 1890, received Seventy Dollars, in full for interest to date. Received July 4th, 1890, Seventy Dollars, Interest in full to date. Received January 4th, 1801, Seventy Dollars, in full f r interest to date

FACE OF NOTE.	Transfer Endorsement and Payments Endorsed on B\CK OF NOTE.

$3000.   Peterboro', Ont., Jan. 4, 1889.
 	
Three years after date, we jointly promise to pay to GEORGE A COX, or order, Three Thousand Dollars, value received, with interest at 6 per cent., payable annually.
 	
No. 3.   HALL, HALL & HALL.
	January 4th, 1890. Received One Hundred and Eighty Dollars, for one years interest, in full to date.
	
	Pay S. EVANS, or order.
	                              GEO. A. COX.
	Received Dec. 4th, 1890 Two Thousand Dollars on within note.
	
	Pay A. L. DAVIS, or order.
	                              S. EVANS.
	
	Received Jan. 4th, 1801. One Hundred and Seventy Dollars, in full to date.

1.—Find the total purchases and sales.   2.—Find the sum of sold and unsold Mdse.   3.—Find the average daily purchases and sales.   4.—Find the net gain or loss.   5.—Find the average daily gain or loss.   6.—Average gain °/₀ on goods sold.   7.—Average gain or loss on total purchases.

1. Mdse.		2. Mdse.		3. Mdse.	
5,000	235	2,350	139	15,000	540
300	975	135	56	6,500	160
250	45	590	75	1,380	1,120
19	560	13	40	450	375
171	75	165	31	758	190
55	35	17	54	139	2,135
28	40	590	180	133	189
162	145	145	150	650	170
175	137	130	70	120	1,561
Inventory, $4,573. Sales for 26 days		Inventory, $2,135. Sales for 15 days		Inventory, $11,250. Sales for 10 days.	

4. Mdse.		5. Mdse.		6. Mdse.	
56,050	4,060	4,730	3,275	5,237	1,249
3,570	5,730	1,310	1,112	365	763
5,234	120	2,150	2,135	1,463	431
320	530	4,320	1,737	1,375	1,321
490	340	130	105	120	3,462
596	420	420	506	375	372
750	732	133	133	542	146
120	231	2,147	731	378	1,375
375	1,642			112	1,112
Inventory, $50,605. Sales for 45 days.		Inventory, $1,060. Sales for 60 days.		Inventory, $4,650. Sales for 90 dys.	

CARP, CHEESE FACTORY, ACCOUNT KEEPING,
AS ARRANGED BY BANNELI. SAWYER.

Month—Date.	Weight of Milk.	Nelson Kidd.	Wm. Argue.	Jas Fenton.	Jas. Johnston.	Wm. Hanly.	S. Evans.	Wm. Rivington.	I. Caldwell.	F. F..ton.	F. Caldwell.	Remarks.
1	140 / 129	126 / 121										
2	145 / 120	130 / 129										
3	160 / 120	160 / 150										
4	160 / 112	165 / 155										
5	150 / 125	130 / 110										
6	152 / 127	120 / 110										
	1640	1606										

NOTE:—The foregoing table illustrates the ruling of the Milk Register in an ordinary Cheese Factory. The milk's weight in pounds is entered morning and evening below the owner's name, and posted with price (where price is fixed) to credit of his account, at the end of each week. We give the form for what it is worth—if anyone has a better method we would be pleased to hear from him.

RAPID CALCULATION OF TRADE PROFITS AND DISCOUNTS.

We have compiled the following tables to aid merchants in readily adding whatever profit they desire and as readily subtracting it. In either the simple or compound table, it may be seen that to deduct the same AMOUNT as was added, a different fraction is required. This new fraction is obtained by adding the numerator and the denominator of the old faction together for a new denominator—the old numerator remains. Example:—Add 40% = 2-5 = $1.40; deduct enough to reduce to cost 2 + 5 = 7 = 2-7. Now then 1-7 off $1.40 is 20c., therefore 2 7 is 40c., which leaves cost price.

REGULAR TABLE OF TRADE PERCENTAGES.
1-SIMPLE.

Cost Price	Increased by part of cost that will make Retail Price.	Increased by the per cent. of cost that will make Retail Price.	Retail Price	Take off part of Retail price to return to Cost.	Take off per cent of Retail price to return to Cost.	Cost price Restored.
$1	1	100 per cent.	2 00	½	50 per cent.	$1
$1	½	50 "	1 50	⅓	33⅓ "	$1
$1	⅓	33⅓ "	1 33⅓	¼	25 "	$1
$1	¼	25 "	1 25	1-5	20 "	$1
$1	1-5	20 "	1 20	1-6	16⅔ "	$1
$1	1-6	16⅔ "	1 16⅔	1-7	14 2-7 "	$1
$1	1-7	14 2-7 "	1 14 2-7	⅛	12½ "	$1
$1	⅛	12½ "	1 12½	1-9	11 1-9 "	$1
$1	1-9	11 1-9 "	1 11 1-9	1-10	10 "	$1
$1	1-10	10 "	1 10	1-11	9 1-11 "	$1
$1	1-11	9 1-11 "	1 09 1-11	1-12	8⅓ "	$1
$1	1-12	8⅓ "	1 08⅓	1-13	7 9-13 "	$1
$1	1-13	7 9-13 "	1 07 9-13	1-14	7 1-7 "	$1
$1	1-14	7 1-7 "	1 07 1-7	1-15	6⅔ "	$1
$1	1-15	6⅔ "	1 06⅔	1-16	6¼ "	$1
$1	1-16	6¼ "	1 06¼	1-17	5 15-17 "	$1
$1	1-17	5 15-17 "	1 05 15-17	1-18	5 5-9 "	$1
$1	1-18	5 5-9 "	1 05 5-9	1-19	5 5-19 "	$1
$1	1-19	5 5-19 "	1 05 5-19	1-20	5 "	$1

2-COMPOUND.

Cost Price.	Increased by the per cent of Cost that will make Retail price.	Increased by the part of Cost that will make Retail Price	Retail Price.	Deduct as follows, to return to Cost Price.	Deduct following per cent, of Retail to return to Cost Price.	Cost Price Restored
$1	⅔	66⅔ per cent.	$1 66⅔	2-5	40 per cent.	$1
$1	3-5	60 "	1 60	3-8	37½ "	$1
$1	5-7	71 3-7 "	1 71 3-7	5-12	41⅔ "	$1
$1	2-5	40 "	1 40	2-7	28 4-7 "	$1
$1	¾	75 "	1 75	3-7	42 6-7 "	$1
$1	4-5	80 "	1 80	4-9	44 4-9 "	$1
$1	5-6	83⅓ "	1 83⅓	5-11	45 5-11 "	$1
$1	⅜	37½ "	1 37½	3-11	27 3-11 "	$1
$1	⅝	62½ "	1 62½	5-13	38 6-13 "	$1
$1	⅞	87½ "	1 87½	7-15	46⅔ "	$1

STOCKS.

The par value of a share of stock is usually $100

A "Bull" is a speculator who sells "short," expecting to make a profit by a decline in prices.

A "Bear" is a speculator who sells "short," expecting to make a profit by a decline in prices.

A "Time Sale" or purchase, made with the intention of speculating in the "margin," or fluctuations in prices, without any design to actually deliver or take the stock, requires no investment, except enough to cover the margin.

A "Put" is the privilege of putting or selling to the one who sells it a certain quantity of specified stock at a given price within a fixed time.

A "Call" is the privilege of calling for or buying a certain stock at a specified price within a given time. The seller of the "put" must be ready to buy, and of the "call" to sell, whenever called upon.

The expression "Long of Stocks" or a "Bull," means that you have bought expecting higher prices.

A "Clique" is a combination of prominent operators, or their brokers, to carry stock up, each bidding higher so as to get control of it.

The expression "Short of Stocks" or a "Bear," means that you have agreed to deliver stocks at some future time, by which time you expect lower prices.

If a member of the Stock Exchange is unable to meet his engagement, the stock which he fails to receive or deliver is "bought in" or "sold out" UNDER THE RULE.

A "Combination" is a number of operators, each placing a certain amount of money in the hands of one of their number, who takes full charge and control of the operation for their joint account, a division being made of the proceeds PRO RATA.

When a stock has passed into the hands of a combination, and the BEARS having sold largely for future delivery, are SHORT of the stock, the members of the combination can of course, make them pay any price they choose for the stock they have agreed to deliver. A large advance is the result, and there is said to be a " corner " in the stock.

STOCK EXCHANGE.

A Stock Exchange is a body of men by whom the change of securities, for valuable considetation, is made.

The members of the "'change" are admitted by election or ballot when vacancies occur, on payment of the admission fee, which in Boston is $2,000, Philadelphia $5,000, New York $10,000. Indeed a single memberbership in the N. Y. Exchange has sold as high as $32,500. There are 1100 members in the " N. Y. 'Change." A membership is transferable, and passes by descent, in case of the holder's death.

Every Association prescribes its own rules and regulations.

A member's word with regard to a contract, made during the session, must be as good as his bond.

SHIPMENT AND MDSE. CO'S.

REMARKS, WITH ILLUSTRATIONS

SHIPMENT Co. represents *your interest* in Mdse. or other property shipped by you to be sold on joint a/c and risk of yourself and other parties ; or it may represent your interest where you receive intelligence that other parties have shipped Mdse. to a third party, and that you are interested.

The term shipment Co. is always and only applied to your interest or share in the shipment.

Debits :—Shipment Co. is debited for your interest and share of the costs in the speculation when the shipment is made.

The persons interested with you are debited for their share of Mdse. and the charges.

Credits :—Ship't Co. is closed to, or by loss and gain. To close before an account sales has been received, you *credit* the Shipment Co. by Balance.

MDSE. CO. is a fictitious name given to goods or other property received by you to sell on joint a/c. and risk.

Debits :—Mdse. Co. is debited to the shipper, when received, for your interest only, and the charges incurred on the full shipment.

Credits :—The shipper is credited for your share in the goods (unless settled for at the time of receiving them,) the same as though bought of him on account.

Mdse. Co is credited for all sales of the goods received.

Each interested party is credited with his share of the net proceeds.

Closing :—Total charges deducted from total sales leaves the *net proceeds*.

In closing debit Mdse. Co. to your commission, to all charges not already posted, to the shippers for their net proceeds, and to loss and gain if you have gained. If you have *lost* then loss and gain is Dr. to Mdse. Co.

When closing, should the goods be but partially sold, Mdse. Co. should be credited *in the Ledger*, by Inventory for your share only, of the Mdse. remaining on hand. The remainder of unsold goods belongs to the shipper.

EXAMPLES SOLVED.

Transaction.

1.—Amos ships Ben. to be sold on joint a/c and risk, each ½ Mdse., invoiced, at $4,000. Insurance, $40.

JOURNAL ENTRY 1.	JOURNAL ENTRY 2.
Ship't Co. Dr....$2015	Mdse, Co. Dr...$2115
Ben. " 2015	To Amos..... $2015 00
To Mdse..... $4000 00	" Bank 100 00
" Cash...... 30 00	

Transaction.

2.—Ben., on receipt of goods pays, per check, $100 freight and cartage.

Transaction.

3.—Ben. sells the Mdse. for $3,250, receiving in payment, check, $1,750, and note at 10 days for balance.

JOURNAL ENTRY 3.	JOURNAL ENTRY 4.
Bills rec. Dr.......$1500	Mdse. Co. Dr..$1135 00
Cash Dr.......... 1750	L. and Gain Dr 480 63
To Mdse. Co...... $3250	To Amos... $1534 38
	" Com... 81 25

4.—Ben. renders Amos an account of sales, charging 2½ % Com.

Total sales.................................... $3250 00
Freight, $100, Com. @ 2½ per c., $81.25......   181 25

Total net proceeds........................... $3068 75

Each one's net proceeds 1534 38
Each one's original ½ of Invoice............. 2014 00

Difference—Each one's net loss .... $ 480 62

Transaction.

    5.—What entry does Amos make on receipt of account sales?

JOURNAL ENTRY 5.

Ben. Dr........................... $1534 38
   To Ship't Co.................... $1534 38

Transaction.

    6.—We will now suppose the Mdse. was not all sold, but that an account sales has been rendered, as above for what has been sold; the Inventory of unsold Mdse. accounts to $2.000. As all the entries would be the same as before, to the time of rendering the account sales, we will just show the last entries, and how to find the net gain or loss of each.

Total sales.................................... $3250 00
Freight, $100, Com. @ 2½ per c., $81 25......   181 25

Total net proceeds........................... $3068 75

Each one's net proceeds of sales.............. 2534 38
Each one's unsold ½ 1000 00

Each one's present interest................... $2534 38
Each one's original ¼........................ 2015 00

Each one's share of net gain.................. $ 519 37

JOURNAL ENTRY 6.   JOURNAL ENTRY 7.

Mdse. Co. Dr..$2135 00 | Ben. Dr..... $1534 38
  To Com ... $ 81 25 | To Ship't Co $1534 38
  " Amos...   1534 38
  " Loss & Gain   519 37

Transaction.

    7.—Amos' entry on receipt of Account Sales.

TO THE STUDENT.

THE highest success is achieved by making the most of one's circumstances, powers and opportunities. Ever bear in mind that no enterprise can be made a permanent success unless it be conducted systematically, as well as honorably. Do nothing without system. Method furnishes the key to all true progress.

In the College you will have every advantage offered you to gain a knowledge of affairs which you will find, in after life, to be invaluable.

When you enter upon your course of study, remember it is worthy of your closest application and best efforts. We give a thoroughly practical business education, and all who master it and heed our advice will be likely to be successful in the battle of life. *Work* must be your motto; honest and well-directed "work" will develop a young man physically, mentally and morally. Labor is a university that does more for its students than Cambridge or Oxford, Harvard or Yale. Determination, earnestness, devotion and courage are the great requirements of success. Remember the College motto, "This one thing I do," should be yours. Concentration of life-purpose is the need of the world. It is also necessary that a young person should possess "tact, push and principle" to reach the top round of the ladder of prosperity. In this direction we endeavor to point the student at the same time that we are imparting the elements of a thorough knowledge of accounts, and penmanship and the ways and means of transacting business. An easy, elegant, legible, expeditious hand-writting is essential to the highest success. Your signature may thus be your best reference.

Strive to make yourself familiar with the most concise and business like forms of expression. Punctuation and neatness enhance greatly the written page. Blots and erasures show a want of care. In learning the science of book-keeping it may at first seem misty and difficult, but to a decided, earnest student difficulties are but incentives to greater endeavor. Others have succeeded by diligence; why not you? Others have spanned the Niagara of achievement; why not you? Remember in every dream of your life or your slumbers that "fortune favors the brave." "Animo et fide," courage and faith, should be the acting impulse of your every heart-throb. Be brave, and in all your work be cheerful.

The earnest student must learn *to do the work*, and the thoughtful teacher will endeavor *to illustrate principles*, not simply to occupy himself in *showing* the student how to work out each entry that may seem new to the learner.

1.—BOOK-KEEPING.

EXPLANATORY NOTES AND ILLUSTRATIONS.

Book-keeping is the recording of business transactions so as to show the true state of each account.

There are two leading methods, namely, Double and Single Entry.

The principal books used are: Day Book, Journal, Ledger and Cash Book. Bill Book, Sales Book, Personal Ledger are used when the business requires them.

A man may select books that are best suited to his business.

An account with a person, a firm or a corporation, is called a Personal Account.

There are two sides to every account; the heading being written in a large heavy hand above the space where the items appear.

There may be a great many different accounts in a set of books, but they are easily divided according to their nature into two classes viz :—1. Fixed accounts, closing To (or By) Balance, which are Resources or Liabilities; 2. Fluctuating Accounts, closing To (or By) Loss and Gain, which are Losses or Gains.

Journalizing is deciding upon and arrranging, the debits and credits in the Journal. The sums of the debits and the credits must be equal.

RULES FOR JOURNALIZING.

DEBITS.	CREDITS.
Debit, what we receive.	Credit, what we give out.
" " costs us value.	" " produces us value.
" the person who gets value from us.	" the person who gives us value.

FURTHER RULES FOR JOURNALIZING.

STOCK, or Proprietors Account.

Debited for liabilities assumed, withdrawals and net losses.

Credited for investment and net gain. The difference shows net investment, present worth or insolvency. Closed "To (or by) balance."

CASH.

Debited for receipts. Credited for payments. The difference shows a resource of the balance on hand. Closed "By Balance."

MDSE.

Debited for cost. Credited for sales. The difference (when the property is all sold or Inventory added to the credit of the account) shows a gain or a loss.—A gain when the credit is in excess; a loss when the debit is in excess. Closed "To (or by) loss and gain.

PERSONAL ACCOUNTS. (Accounts with persons.)

Debited when they become debtor to us and we pay them.

Credited when we become debtor to them and they pay us.

The difference shows a resource or liability consisting of the amount we owe them or they owe us—a resource when the debit is in excess, a liability when the credit is in excess. Closed "To (or by) balance."

EXPENSE.

Debited for cost or outlay. Credited for returns (if any). The difference shows a loss. Closed, "by loss and gain."

BILLS RECEIVABLE.

Debited for others notes and "acceptances" when received. Credited when they are paid or disposed of. The difference shows a resource of other's papers on hand. Closed, " By balance.'

BILLS PAYABLE.

Credited with our notes and "acceptances" when issued. Debited when paid or redeemed. The difference shows a liability of our paper unpaid. Closed "To balance."

REAL ESTATE.

Debited for cost and expense. Credited for Sales, Rents and Returns. The difference under same conditions as Mdse. The account shows a gain or a loss.

INTEREST, DISCOUNT AND PREMIUM.

Debited for cost or when allowed to others. Credited for what it produces, or when allowed to us. The difference shows a gain, when credit is in excess; a loss when the debit is in excess. Closed ''To (or by) loss and gain."

INSURANCE.

Debited for cost. Credited for whatever it produces, or allowances in our favor. The difference shows a gain or a loss. Conditions same as in Interest. Closed, " To (or by) loss and gain."

SHIPMENTS.

Debited for cost value of goods shipped and for all other costs. Credited for returns or net proceeds. The difference shows a loss or a gain. Conditions same as Mdse. Closed " To (or by) loss and gain."

CONSIGNMENTS.

Debited for charges and costs. Credited for sales. The difference shows the net proceeds due to the Consignor.

COMMISSION.

Debited for cost. Credited for what it produces, or allowances in our favor. The difference shows a loss or a gain. Conditions same as Interest. Closed, " To (or by) loss and gain."

STORAGE.

Debited for cost. Credited for what it produces. The difference shows a gain or a loss. Conditions same as Interest. Closed, " To (or by) loss and gain."

FIXTURES, STORE AND SHOP FIXTURES.

Debited for cost. Credited for proceeds. The difference will generally show a loss. A gain may possibly arise. Conditions same as Mdse. Closed " To (or by) loss and gain."

BANK, RAILWAY AND OTHER STOCKS.

Debited for costs and assessments. Credited for sales and dividends. The difference shows a gain or a loss. Conditions same as Mdse. Closed " To (or by) loss and gain."

MORTGAGE RECEIVABLE.

Debited, credited and conditions same as Bills Receivable. Closed " By balance."

MORTGAGE PAYABLE.

Debited, credited and conditions same as Bills Payable. Closed " To balance."

LOSS AND GAIN.

Debited for losses. Credited for gains, either direct or through the closing of representative accounts. The difference shows a net gain or a net loss—a net gain if the credit is in the excess ; a net loss when the debit side is in the excess. Closed "To (or by) Stock," or "To (or by) paitner's name."

PARTNERS' ACCOUNTS.

Similar to Stock. Each partner is debited to liabilities assumed by him, his withdrawals, and for his private account, if a loss. Credited for his investment and private account if a gain. The difference shows his net interest in the business—if the credit side is in excess, his present worth ; if the debit is in excess, his insolvency or indebtedness to the business. Closed "To (or by) balance."

PRIVATE ACCOUNT.

If there is a single proprietor, debit his withdrawals from the business, of money, mdse., property or value of any kind. Credit with salary or allowance. Close into his capital account.

An account is an item or a collection of items under a distinct title.

The balance of an account is the excess of one side above the other.

When the debit side of an account is the larger, the account has a debit balance ; When the credit side is the larger, it has a credit balance.

Accounts are divided into two classes : *Fixed and Fluctuating.*

A fixed account is one representing property having a fixed value as Cash, Bills Receivable, J Jones, etc.

A Fluctuating account is one representing property having a variable value, or representing expenses, as Mdse, Real Estate, Rent, etc.

FIXED ACCOUNTS stand for either Resources or Libialities ; FLUCTUATING ACCOUNTS stand for either Losses or Gains.

A RESOURCE, also called an asset, is anything one *owns*, and a LIABILITY is anything one *owes* ; it is a debt.

Liabilities are either inside or outside.

An Inside Liability is an obligation due to parties interested in the gains and losses of a business.

An Outside Liability is an obligation due to parties not interested in the gains and losses of a business.

A Loss occurs in business when goods are lost, stolen, destroyed or disposed of for less than their cost or value.

A GAIN occurs when goods are found, or are sold for more than their cost price.

GROSS LOSS is the sum of all the losses during a given time; GROSS GAIN is the sum of all the gains during a given time.

NET GAIN is the Gross Gain with the Gross Loss subtracted.

NET LOSS is the Gross Loss with the Gross Gain subtracted.

NET INVESTMENT is the difference between the sum of the Resources and the sum of the Liabilities of a firm, on the commencement of a term of business. NET WORTH *minus* RESOURCES = Liabilities in a business at any time.

PRESENT WORTH is what a firm is worth at the present time: It is found by subtracting the outside Liabilities from the Resources; as is done in the Balance Account in the Ledger. Another method is to add the Net Gain or subtract the Net Loss, from the Net Investment; as is done in the Stock Account in the Ledger.

INSOLVENCY is the financial condition of one, who not only cannot pay his debts, but whose outside liabilities are greater than his Resources:

PRESENT INSOLVENCY may therefore be found by subtracting the Resources from the Outside Liabilities.

AN INVENTORY is a list of property (personal or real) of which a person or firm is possessed at the time of closing the Ledger, or at any other stated time. What is generally known as "Stock Taking" is the process of finding Inventories, or the value of goods on hand.

When Journalizing be careful to debit bank when you make a deposit; and credit bank when you issue a check. This may hereafter be dealt with differently.

A DRAFT is an unconditional written order addressed by one person to a second, requesting him to pay a specified sum of money to himself, or to a third party.

A Draft may be drawn " At Sight," " After Sight," " After Date,' or " On Demand."

A SIGHT DRAFT is payable 3 days after acceptance *i. e.* after the day upon which the payer agrees to pay.

CREDIT the person upon whom you draw a draft.

DEBIT the person who draws a draft upon you.

OUR ACCEPTANCE we call BILLS PAYABLE : because we agree, by our acceptance, to pay it.

ANOTHER'S ACCEPTANCE, in our favor, we call BILLS RECEIVABLE, because we expect to receive the money for it.

When a DRAFT or promissory note, bearing interest, is DISCOUNTED, the interest up to date of maturity must be added, and the discount calculated on the sum.

When a firm begins business, debit "capital account" to what is owing, and credit capital by what is owned and invested.

FOOTINGS mean sums of columns. To foot up a column is to add it up.

POSTING is transferring entries from the Journal to their proper headings or accounts in the Ledger ; and when the posting is finished the total debits and total credits should be equal. To show that this is the case, each amount in the Ledger must be added or footed up, and the sum of the debits should equal the sum of the credits. A paper or statement showing this is called a Trial Balance ; and is taken as presumptive evidence of the correctness of the Ledger.

QUESTIONS
ON WORK COVERED BY FIRST EXAMINATION.

What is book-keeping? How many methods are there? Name them? Name the principal books? What is a Personal Account? Name the different kinds of accounts? How does each class or kind close? What is Journalizing? Give the rules for Journalizing? Why is the debit side of Cash Account always equal to or larger than the credit? Why is the credit side of B. Pay. always equal to or larger than the debit? Examine carefully each amount? What is an account? What is the balance of an account? What is the credit balance? What is a resource, a liability, a loss and a gain? What do you mean by inside and outside liabilities? What do you understand by gross gain and gross loss? What is net loss? Net gain? Net investment? Net worth? What is present insolvency? What is an inventory? What do you mean by "Stock Taking"? What is a draft? What is an acceptance? Explain the terms "at sight," "on demand"? Give the rules for Journalizing drafts? How is the discount found on an interest bearing note? What Journal entry is made for liabilities on beginning business? What are footings? What is posting? What is a trial balance? What kind of evidence does it furnish as to the correctness of the work?

2.—BOOKS.

The following rule will guide you in naming books. Any book is a principal book if you post from it direct to the Ledger, and any book is an auxiliary one from which you do not post direct but which you keep for easy reference, or the like.

The following are descriptions of each of the books heretofore enumerated. Study carefully.

DAY-BOOK.

This book contains a statement of all business transactions as they occur. The entry being made at the time when the transaction took place and should include,

(1) The date of the transaction.
(2) The name of the person or account.
(3) The commodity received or given.
(4) The price, quantity etc of Mdse., bot. or sold.
(5) The terms of payment.

TO CORRECT AN ERROR.

This is a book of original entry *i. e.* the entry is made in it at the time when the transaction took place, and in it erasing is not excusable (see books as evidence in Court.) If the entry is wrong and has not already been transferred mark it "Void, corrected page—," then on the page mentioned make the entry as it ought to appear, at the same time referring to the page where the error was made. All corrections must leave the entry legible.

NOTE: For form of this book see Set 1. Primary.

JOURNAL.

This book is generally ruled the same as a Day Book and contains the name of accounts to be Debited and Credited taken from the Day-Book. The debits and credits must be equal in each journal entry. The most difficult part though not the whole of the art of Double Entry Book-keeping, is in journalizing. An entry in this book includes (1) The date. (2) The accounts to be charged or credited. (3) The sum of the transaction.

TO CORRECT AN ERROR.

If the Journal is used simply as a medium of passing entries from the other book or books to the Ledger, an occasional erasure of a word or a figure is not condemned in practice.

Where the entire entry is wrong it is best to mark it "void" correcting with another entry or to make a cross entry without changing the first. To make a cross entry, see page 27.

NOTE: For form of this book see Set 1, Primary.

CASH BOOK.

This book is kept to show the amount of cash received during a day, week, month or longer period, the amount of cash paid out during the period and the balance, if any, remaining on hand. The left side of the book shows the "receipts" and the right side shows the "disbursements" or sums paid out.

The difference between the sums of sides will show the balance of Cash on hand, at any date desired, same as the Cash account in Ledger, when it is kept there.

Every evening you should see that the balance shown in the C. B. agrees with the amount of cash on hand—this is called "proving the cash." The balance on hand at the close of each week should be put on the *credit side in red ink* and then brought down to the *debit side in black ink*—this is called "balancing the C. B."

Whenever cash is received the amount should be entered on the left or debit side of the cash book, giving first the date, next the title of the account to be credited, next the explanatory remarks and finally the amount. Whenever Cash is paid out you should enter on the right or credit side of the C. B. the title of the account to be debited, the explanatory remarks and the amount. The C. B. may be proved by adding each side with lead pencil and finding the difference, which difference must agree with cash on hand. This is also a book of original entry and therefore the entries should be made as they occur and with sufficient explanatory remarks to present the transaction correctly before the mind. Erasures must be avoided. As you cannot pay out more cash than you receive, so the debit or "received" side should always be equal to or greater than the credit or "paid out" side. The difference, if any, should equal the cash on hand, and should be placed on the credit side in red ink " By Balance." After footing up both sides and "ruling off," the Balance should be brought down in black ink to the debit side, last column, with the date of the next business day in the margin.

Note ; For form of this book see Set 1. Junior.

LEDGER.

This book contains the names of accounts with persons with whom you are dealing, of property in which you are dealing, and cost or expense accounts of the business. One account is open for each person, kind of property, or class of expense, and all the transactions affecting each account are carried or posted from the Journal to the proper account in this book. The left side being the debit or charge side and the right side being the credit side. The entries to this book come mainly direct from the Journal and C. B., though sometimes partly from the Sales and Invoice books. This book is the epitome of all transactions, properly classified for convenient reference, and just distribution amongst the debtors and creditors. The result of a man's business is here found, from which a still more condensed statement may be taken for purposes of comparison with past, and guidance in future years.

ORDER OF OPENING LEDGER.

(1) Open Stock or Partner's accounts.
(2) Open Cash, Mdse., Bills Receivable and Payable.
(3) Open Personal accounts.
(4) Open accounts such as Freight, Salary, etc.

ORDER OF CLOSING THE LEDGER.

(1) Take off a Trial Balance.
(2) Open Loss and Gain and Balance accounts.
(3) Close those accounts which show a loss or gain into Loss and Gain account.
(4) Close those accounts which show a resource or liability into Balance account.
(5) Close Loss and Gain into Stock.
(6) Close Private account into Stock.
(7) Close Stock into Balance.

STUDENT'S KEY TO CLOSING THE LEDGER.

1. Fixed
   - (a) Dr. Balances are Resourses, Cash, B. Rec.
   - (b) Cr. Balances are Liabilities, B. Pay. Personal accounts.
   } Closed to or by Balance.

2. Fluctuating
   - (a) Dr. Balances are Losses { Merchandise, Real Estate, Bank Stock, Int. and Dis, Expense
   - (b) Cr. Balances are Gains
   } Closed To or By Loss and Gain.

TO MAKE A CROSS ENTRY

The following rule must be observed :

Debit the account or accounts that have been wrongly credited, or that should have been debited, and credit the account or accounts that have been wrongly debited, or that should have been credited.

NOTE : For form of Ledger see Set 1, Primary.

BILL BOOK.

This book is kept to show the particulars of all notes and drafts received or given out. When the entry for a note or draft issued or received has been properly made in the Journal or Sales Book, you should next enter the particulars of the bill as to date, time, drawer, indorser, amount, when payable and so forth in the Bill Book. *To get the date of maturity of any paper always add three days of grcae.* When a bill has been paid, discounted or otherwise disposed, of a "memo" should be made of it in the column marked "when and how disposed of." Double red ink lines should be drawn through the figures representing the face of a note as soon as it has been paid or disposed of. Care should be taken in finding the date of maturity of paper. Posting is not usually done from the B. B.

NOTE : For form of this book see Wholesale Set 5.

JOURNAL-DAY BOOK.

This book as its name implies is a union of D. B. and J. The Journal entry is first given in medium sized writing. Then follows the description, explanation or day-book entry in a smaller hand. This book saves time and labor in account keeping and saves money in buying books.

NOTE : For form of this book see Set 1, Junior.

INVOICE BOOK.

There are at least two ways of keeping this book, namely, by using a large manilla scrap-book in which to paste the invoices as received.

Money columns should be ruled to the right of each page so that the sum of each purchase or invoice may be therein extended and added, and at the close of the month posted *in total* to the debit of Mdse. at the same time separated, crediting the different accounts which require it. All invoices should be folded up to the depth of a quarter page and when pasted in position, the prices of their contents endorsed on the side lying upward. Another plan is to file away the invoices as other papers are filed and enter an abstract of each in a book. This method is just as convenient as the former method except that it is found necessary to examine the document when you turn it up, whereas by the former method when you examine the endorsement should that not be satisfactory you can open the paper and examine it without further trouble.

NOTE : For form of this book see Wholesale Set 5.

SALES BOOK.

As the name indicates, the sales of Mdse. on account are extended in this book. The date, name, items, terms of sale and the amounts should be carefully noted. The purchasers are debited or charged direct from this book with the amount of their purchase, and Mdse. is credited with the sum of the sales every time the books are posted, which is usually monthly.

When sales are made for part cash, the entry should be made complete in this book, and the balance *received in cash*, put into the C. B. Cash sales are extended in both the C. B. and the Sales Book, but posted direct to the Ledger from the Sales Book. It is from the Sales Book that itemized statements of accounts are made out. Some Accountants enter cash sales in the C. B. alone and post direct from that book, sometimes keeping a special column and posting in total weekly or monthly. We prefer putting all the Sales through the Sales Book. There are many methods employed to keep this book satisfactorily in large business houses. (1) By having two books, one labelled "Monday, Wednesday, Friday," the other labelled, "Tuesday, Thursday, Saturday." The advantage in using two books is when the entries are being made in one of them the other may be posted up. (2) By keeping the Sales Book in leaves until a sufficient number are filled to form a book, when they may be bound together in book form. Thus the clerks as they fill the pages hand them in to the Ledger-keeper who posts the entries and files away the leaves. (3) By the use of tissue paper and carbon thus taking a copy that will answer for posting even though the Sales Book may be engaged, being written up.

NOTE: For form of this book see Wholesale Set 5.

SPECIAL ACCOUNT BOOKS.

The following books are comonly used for ease, and economy of time, either in posting or in rendering accounts, (*a*) Special Column Journal, (*b*) Personal Ledger, (*c*) Commission Sales Ledger.

(*a*) SPECIAL COLUMN JOURNAL.

This book explains itself. It is a Journal having several money columns, into which may be placed, for example, in one column, ' Mdse. Dr." in another all "Cash Dr." and so on as illustrated. The posting may then be done periodically (generally monthly) carrying the total of "Mdse. Dr." to the debit of Mdse. account in the Ledger and then the debit of Cash and so on. All other items must be entered in the Sundries Dr. and Cr. columns and afterwards posted separately.

NOTE: For form of this book see Retail Set 1.

(*b*) THE PERSONAL LEDGER.

This is a book ruled like a Journal, into which are entered accounts with customers. Generally this is written up from the entries in Order Book remaining unpaid at the close of the day. As many items as possible are written on each line and when value is received on ac. it is credited "By Cash" or otherwise as the case may be, and extending the figures to the right hand or credit column.

NOTE: For form of this book see Retail Set 1.

(*c*) THE COMMISSION SALES LEDGER.

This is a book ruled like a Personal Ledger but both left and right hand pages are used for each account. When a consignment is sold or or partly sold the proper entry is made on the right hand side crediting the consignment by the commodity received.

NOTE: For form of this book see Consignments Set 2.

POINTS.

The following points are considered of sufficient importance to make special mention of them.

PRIVATE LEDGER.

This is a Ledger into which the proprietor or partners may enter investments, keeping it under lock and key, and thus avoiding unnecessary exposure. When beginning business the first or investment entry may be made in this book; and when withdrawals or additional investments are made the necessary entry may also be made here. Mdse., Loss and Gain accounts may also be kept in this book, and in fact any account deemed necessary for the sake of privacy.

BOOKS AS EVIDENCE IN COURT.

The following points must be established:—
1. By whom the entries were made.
2. That these books produced are the regular account books.
3. That all, or at least some of the goods have been delivered.
4. That he is honest and accurate in his account keeping— shewn by those who have dealt with him.
5. That the books are books of original entry.

ACCOUNTS WITH BRANCH HOUSES.

These are treated like an ordinary Merchandise account, debiting the Branch for whatever is delivered to it, and crediting it by whatever is received from it. In "Stock-taking" it should be credited by Inventory (unsold goods), and the difference in the sides of the account will then show a loss or a gain. It is debited for all costs. Credit Branch with any goods returned. Branch should be debited when it reports a net gain, and credited when it reports a net loss—the latter is *generally* the entry that has to be made. The Branch should keep an account with the "Head Office," or "Principal House," and when it (the Branch) purchases goods, the Principal House should be credited and not the parties from whom purchase was made. All bills are usually settled by the Head Office.

"BAD DEBTS ACCOUNT."—How to write off.

In every business bad debts accumulate. And when it is found that accounts are not collected it is better to write them off than to be carrying them forward or allowing them to stand open and unchanged upon the face of the Ledger. Every year at the time of stock taking and closing of Ledger, you should go carefully through the Ledger making a note of all the accounts which you think are worthless and then make the following entry:—

Bad Debts Acct., Dr.
To Personal Accts, Cr.

If a promissory note is found worthless write it off as follows:

Bad Debts, Dr.
To Bills Rec., Cr.

If a personal Acct. previously closed into Bad Debts shall be subsequently paid make an entry as follows:
Cash Dr.
To Bad Debts, Cr.

When closing the Ledger accounts, close "Bad Debts Acct." into Loss and Gain.

TRANSFERRING ACCOUNTS FROM ONE LEDGER TO ANOTHER.

Let the old Ledger be called "A" and the new one "B." Close all resource accounts By Balance Ledger B. Folio――; close all liability accounts To Balance Ledger B. Folio――. Open the ac. in Ledger B., putting all To Balances on the Credit and all By Balances on the debit side of Ledger B. Index each account after transferring.

PLANT ACCOUNT.

The "Plant" account in a business represents the machinery, tools, etc., employed in the manufacture of goods or the prosecution of a craft. The account is charged with the cost and credited with the wear and tear on machinery, charging Loss and Gain with the wear and tear every time the Ledger is closed. Or again:—by taking an Inventory of Plant the amount might be credited by the amount of Inventory and then closed into Loss and Gain account.

EXHIBITING SETTLEMENTS IN THE LEDGER.

Without ruling off, every time an account is settled it may be indicated by placing a red ink check thus √ opposite the items, or dates on each side when the settlement was effected. The Ledger should not be ruled except when balancing. Another plan is to put the first letter of the alphabet (A) opposite the items instead of the check mark; and when the second settlement is made put the second letter (B) instead of the check mark. And so on C.D., &c.

QUESTIONS
ON WORK COVERING SECOND EXAMINATION.

How do you distinguish principal books? What does the Day Book contain? What should an entry include? How should an entry be corrected in the D. B.? Why should erasures be avoided? What does the Journal contain? What does an entry in it include? What is the most dificult part of D. E. book-keeping? When is the erasure of a word or figure in the Journal admissible? When is it best to make a cross entry in the Journal? For what purpose is the Cash Book kept? What does the left side show? The right side? What is the difference between the sides? How often should the C. B. be "proved"? How often should it be balanced? In what colored ink should the balance be entered? What should be done after balancing? Into what column should the figures be carried? What is the Ledger? What does it contain? On which side are charges entered? From what books do entries come chiefly, to this book? Why are accounts arranged as they are in the Ledger? Why do men require abstracts and statements from the Ledger? Give the order of opening the ledger? How do you proceed in closing the Ledger after having taken off a trial balance? Which is the last account closed? Write out the student's key to closing the Ledger? Give the principle of making a cross entry? Why is a B. B. used? Is the B. B. an auxilliary or a principal book? How is the date of maturity of a bill found? How do you indicate the payment or disposal of a bill? How is the J. D. B. formed? For what purposes are different sized styles of writing used? What is the advantage of using this book? What is an Invoice Book used for? How many ways are there of keeping it? Describe one way? What does the S. B. contain? What should be noted in each entry? Is posting done from this book? If so how often? Explain the entry of a sale for which part cash has been received? How about cash sales? From which book are itemized statements of account made out? Describe the best method you know of keeping a Sales Book? Name three special account books? Describe each? What,and of what use is a Private Ledger? What points must be established so that books may be taken as evidence in court? What accounts are kept with Branch Houses? How is an account with a Branch treated? What should be done when a Branch reports a gain? What credit should be made by a Branch when goods are purchased? What plan do you use to write off "bad debts"? Describe the method of transferring accounts from an old to a new Ledger.

3.—DAY BOOK ENTRIES JOURNALIZED.

NOTE.—The Capital letters placed after the number of the Example stand for the names of the books in which the entry should be made. Sometimes an entry should appear in several books but should be posted from one only.

TRANSACTIONS IN CASH.

Remarks :—Debit Cash when received, Credit Cash when paid out.

Example 1. Bot. for cash 25 bbls. Flour @ $6.25—(J. and C.B.)

EXAMPLE 1.—JOURNAL ENTRY.

L F	Mdse. Dr........................	156 25	
L F	To Cash		156 25

Example 2. Bot. of D. J. McLennan for cash, 60 bbls. Flour @ $6.40 —(J.-C.B.)

EXAMPLE 2.—JOURNAL ENTRY.

L F	Mdse. Dr........................	384 00	
L F	To Cash		384 00

Example 3. Sold for cash 6 bbls. Flour @ $7.10—(S.B.-C.B.)

EXAMPLE 3.—JOURNAL ENTRY.

L F	Cash Dr....	42 60	
L F	To Mdse....		42 60

Example 4. Sold C. Clemes & Son for cash 25 bbls. Flour @ $7.00— (S.B.-C.B.)

EXAMPLE 4.—JOURNAL ENTRY.

L F	Cash Dr....	175 00	
L F	To Mdse		175 00

TRANSACTIONS WITH BANK.

Remarks:—Debit Bank when you deposit cash. Credit Bank when you issue a cheque.

Example 5. Deposited in Bank of Toronto, Cash $6,000—(C.B.)

EXAMPLE 5.—JOURNAL ENTRY.

L F	Bank of Toronto, Dr................	6000	00		
L F	To Cash.........			6000	00

Example 6. Withdrew from Bank of Toronto per c'k in favor of self, $500—(C.B.)

EXAMPLE 6.—JOURNAL ENTRY.

L F	Cash Dr.....	500	00		
L F	To Bank of Toronto			500	00

Example 7. Gave H. Jackson a check to settle a/c $125—(J.)

EXAMPLE 7.—JOURNAL ENTRY.

L F	H. Jackson, Dr.....	125	00		
L F	To Bank			125	00

Example 8. Bot. of Dundas & Flavelle for c'k, Mdse. per invoice $275.—(C.B.)

EXAMPLE 8 —JOURNAL ENTRY.

L F	Mdse. Dr.	275	00		
L F	To Bank			275	00

Example 9. Sold G. W. Bell for check Mdse, amounting to $877.30 —(S.B.)

EXAMPLE 9.—JOURNAL ENTRY.

L F	Cash Dr.........................	877	30		
L F	To Mdse....			877	30

Example 10. Withdrew what cash I had in B'k of Toronto—(C.B.)

EXAMPLE 10.—JOURNAL ENTRY.

L F	Cash Dr............................	$100	00		
L F	To Bank of Toronto			$100	00

TRANSACTIONS ON ACCOUNT.

Remarks :—Debit persons when you give them anything without receiving any equivalent at the time. Credit persons who give you something for which you return no equivalent at the time.

Example 11. Sold J. Graham on a/c 400 yds. Gingham @ 15c = $60.00 (J.)

EXAMPLE 11.—JOURNAL ENTRY

L F	J. Graham, Dr......................	60	00		
L F	To Mdse....			60	00

Example 12. Sold J. Kennedy on 60 days' credit 400 yds. Tricot @ 72c = $288—(J.)

EXAMPLE 12.—JOURNAL ENTRY.

L F	J. Kennedy, Dr.....................	288	00		
L F	To Mdse....			288	00

Example 13. Received from J. Graham cash in full of a/c $60—(C.B.)

EXAMPLE 13.—JOURNAL ENTRY.

L F	Cash Dr.........	60	00		
L F	To J. Graham.....................			60	00

Example 14. Received from J. Kennedy cash on a/c $200—(C.B.)

EXAMPLE 14.—JOURNAL ENTRY.

L F	Cash Dr............................	200	00		
L F	To J. Kennedy......			200	00

Example 15. Bot. of Bradburn & Co. on a/c 10 cases, 14,080 yds. Prints at 8½c per yd., $1196.80—(J.)

EXAMPLE 15.—JOURNAL ENTRY.

L F	Mdse. Dr............................	1196	80		
L F	To Bradburn & Co.			1196	80

Example 16. Paid Bradburn & Co. cash on a/c $1000—(C.B.)

EXAMPLE 16.—JOURNAL ENTRY.

L F	Bradburn & Co., Dr................	1000	00		
L F	To Cash........			1000	00

PROMISSORY NOTES.

A PROMISSORY NOTE is a written promise, to pay, unconditionally, and at all events, a certain sum of money, at a specified time.

THE MAKER is the person who signed it, promising to pay the amount at maturity.

THE PAYEE is the person to whom the money is promised to be paid.

MATURITY is the date upon which the note should be paid.

The essentials of a good promissory note are as follows:

(1) The promise must be to pay *money*.
(2) The *time* must be *definite*.
(3) It must be in *writing*.
(4) The *sum* must be stated.
(5) There must be *consideration*.
(6) The person making must be legally accountable for payment at maturity.

Notes are either Negotiable or Non-negotiable.

A note is non-negotiable when made payable only to the payee.

A negotiable note may be drawn to "order" or "bearer."

A Negotiable note is transferable without indorsement if the word "bearer" appears in it, and by indorsement if it is payable to "order" of payee.

Indorsements may be (1) "in blank," (2) "in full," (3) "restrictvily" or (4) "qualified."
Examples of each kind of indorsement mentioned above.
(1) J. Jones.
(2) Pay to A. B. or order.
   J. Jones.
(3) Pay to A. B. only
   J. Jones.
(4) Without recourse to me.
   J. Jones.

Indorsements are made in the regular course of trade for these purposes :
(1) To transfer them.
(2) To secure payment.
(3) To acknowledge partial payment.

If you are a purchaser of a negotiable note you may be called upon to show :
(1) That you gave value for it before its maturity.
(2) That at the time of purchase you were not aware of any claim or condition affecting the validity of the note.

A note not paid at maturity is protested in order to hold the endorsers.

Interest may be reckoned on the three days of grace. No days of grace are allowed on "demand" notes. If a note falls due on Sunday or a public holiday (bank holiday) then it is payable the day following.

For notes drawn at 4 months on October, 28, 29, 30 or 31st would fall due on the same day. Why? Because notes drawn at so many months after date, mean calendar months and February having only 28 days the paper must mature the 3rd day of March.

When a note matures, it must be presented for payment during business hours at the place mentioned on the face of it. If no place is mentioned, present at maker's residence or business office.

If a note is not presented for payment on the very day on which it matures the holder looses his remedy against the endorsers, but the maker is still liable.

When a note is paid it should be marked "paid." The interest on an interest-bearing note is regarded as a part of the debt of the maker and is reckoned from the date of its making. A note generally bears interest from the date of its maturity to the date when it is paid.

A note signed by two or more persons beginning "we promise etc." is termed a *joint note*.

The makers are jointly liable.

If the note, signed by two or more persons, contains the words " I promise, etc." or " We jointly and severally promise, etc." is called a *joint and several* note.

An accommodation, is a note signed or endorsed by a friend to admit (by virtue of two acceptable names) of its being discounted at the Bank to raise funds.

Or, two persons may exchange notes payable to each other, which, when endorsed may be discounted, and when due may be redeemed by the makers respectively, if one has not become insolvent in the meantime.

TRANSACTIONS WITH NOTES.

Remarks :—Debit others' notes received as Bills Rec. Credit your own notes issued as Bills Payable.

Example 17.   Bot. of D. J. McLennan on our note @ 10 dys. 6 bbls. Flour @ $7.00—(J.-B.B.)

EXAMPLE 17.—JOURNAL ENTRY.

L F	Mdse. Dr.	42 00	
L F	To Bills Pay.................		42 00

Example 18.   Sold J. W. Wallace on his note at 4 mos., 2 cases Prints 2873 yds. @ 12c=$344.76—(S.B.-B.B.)

EXAMPLE 18.—JOURNAL ENTRY.

L F	Bills Rec. Dr......	344 76	
L F	To Mdse.		344 76

Example 19.   Bot. of Pillow, Hearsy & Co., Montreal, Mdse. per Invoice $728.22, for which I hand them in payment J. Wallace's note, received to-day, and my own note for bal.—(J.-B.B.)

EXAMPLE 19.—JOURNAL ENTRY.

L F	Mdse. Dr........................	728	22		
L F	To Bills Rec.....................			344	76
L F	" " Pay.......................			383	46

Example 20.—Paid our note in favor of D. J. McLennan by giving him goods from shop worth $42.00—(S.B.-B.B.)

EXAMPLE 20.—JOURNAL ENTRY.

L F	Bills Pay. Dr.....................	42	00		
L F	To Mdse......			42	00

TRANSACTIONS IN PART PAYMENT.

Remarks :—When only part payment is received for the sale of goods—Debit what you receive for its value, and Debit the person receiving the goods for the part unpaid. When purchasing—credit the person from whom you receive the goods by the amount unpaid.

Example 21. Sold J. Kennedy 5 cases, 7,050 yds. Print @ 11c = $775.50 Received in payment, Cash $275.50, bal. on a/c $500— (S.B., C.B.)

EXAMPLE 21.—JOURNAL ENTRY.

	Cash Dr.......................	275	50		
	J. Kennedy Dr.................	500			
	To Mdse......................			775	50

Example 22. Bot. of Thomas Robertson & Co., Montreal, Que.—

    1 Car load Pig Iron 24,365 lbs. @ 3c..... $ 730.95
    1 " Bar Iron 24,537 lbs. @ 5c..... 1226.85
    1 Lot (asst'd) Steam and Gas Fittings 475.25

                                                 $2433.05

Gave in payment my notes at 2, 3 and 4 mos. for $600; $600, and $800. Cash for bal., $433.05.

EXAMPLE 22.—JOURNAL ENTRY.

Mdse. Dr....................	2433	05	
To Bills Pay.................		2000	00
" Cash........................		433	05

Example 23. Bot. of the Pbro. L. & I. Works 50 doz. Locks (complete) @ $4.10 = $205. Gave in payment my note at 30 days for $100, balance to remain on open a/c $105.

EXAMPLE 23.—JOURNAL ENTRY.

Mdse. Dr......................	205	00	
To Bills Pay...................		100	00
" P. L. & I. Works.............		105	00

Example 24. Sold Jas. Hope & Co. Mdse. amounting to $100. Received in payment check, cash and note @ 30 days, each ¼ of the amount of sale, the bal. to remain on a/c.

EXAMPLE 24.—JOURNAL ENTRY.

Jas. Hope Dr.................	25	00	
Cash Dr.......................	50	00	
Bills Rec. Dr..................	25	00	
To Mdse...................		100	00

TRANSACTIONS IN DRAFTS.

Remarks.—A Draft is an unconditional written order addressed by one person to a second, requesting him to pay a specified sum of money to a third or to himself.

The Drawer is the person who signs the Draft.

The Drawee is the person on whom the Draft is made.

The Payee is the person who is to receive payment.

The time is usually specified as follows:—At Sight, After Sight, After Date, or On Demand.

The one who is requested to pay the Draft (the Drawee), is not liable until he accepts it, which he does by writing across the face of it his name, the date, and when he intends making payment. When this is done he is called the Acceptor, and the Draft the Acceptance.

Acceptance may be General, Special, or Qualified.

A General acceptance is made by the Acceptor writing across the face of the Bill the date, his name, the word "Accepted."

Special requires word "Accepted," date, name, place of payment.

Qualified acceptance is either partial or conditional: partial when the Drawee agrees to pay a portion of the amount, or varies the time of payment; and conditional when the Bill is made payable only after a named event happens.

If the Draft is not accepted the Drawer should be notified immediately. If it has been accepted but is not paid at maturity, it should be protested, a notary public sending notices to all parties to it, so as to hold the endorsers.

An accepted Draft becomes in effect, the same as a Promissory Note; the Acceptor has the same relation to it as the Maker has to a note.

RULES FOR JOURNALIZING DRAFTS.

1. Debit the party who draws on you.
2. Credit the party on whom you draw.

	For Sight & Demand.	After Sight or Date.
1. Drawer's Entry.	Payee Dr. To Drawee.	Payee Dr. To Drawee.
2. Drawee's Entry.	Drawer Dr. To Cash.	Drawer Dr. To Bills Pay.
3. Payee's Entry	Cash Dr. To Drawer.	Bills Rec. Dr. To Drawer.
4. Drawer's Entry, when Draft is drawn in his own favor.	Cash Dr. To Drawer.	Bills Rec. Dr. To Drawer.
5. Drawee's Entry when he *pays by check* instead of Cash.	Drawer Dr. To Bank.	

(SIGHT DRAFT.)
$100.00   OTTAWA, Jan. 9th, 1888.
At Sight pay to the order of Scott & Raney (*Payee*), One Hundred Dollars, value received, and charge to account of
                                          WILSON EVANS (*Drawer*)
To T. DOLAN (*Drawee*),
      PETERBOROUGH, ONT.

DRAWER.

1. Wilson Evans' entry when he gives the draft to Scott & Raney to apply on account.............. } Scott & Raney Dr. $100
   To T. Dolan Cr. 100

PAYEE.

2. Scott & Raney's entry when they received the draft from Wilson Evans to apply on account...... } Cash Dr. $100
   To W. Evans 100

DRAWEE.

3. T. Dolan's entry at time of accepting and paying the draft in cash.......... } Wilson Evans, Dr. $100.
   To Cash, Cr. $100.

NOTE.—Acceptance must be written on the face of above draft by T. Dolan, before the bill is negotiable, similar to the following:—

Accepted Ontario Bank, Peterborough, T. Dolan, Jan. 12, 1888.

Example 25. Sold J. M. Hawkins on his acceptance @ 3 days' sight 50 bbls. Flour @ $6.50 = $325—(S.B.-B.B.)

EXAMPLE 25.—JOURNAL ENTRY.

L F	Bills Rec. Dr....................	325	00	
L F	To Mdse................			325	00

Example 26. Received Cash for J. M. Hawkins' Acceptance $325— (C.B.-B.B.)

EXAMPLE 26.—JOURNAL ENTRY.

L F	Cash Dr...................	325	00	
L F	To Bills Rec....................			325	00

Example 27. Drew on S. H. Blake, Toronto, at 60 days' sight to balance account, $100—(B.B.-J.)

EXAMPLE 27.—JOURNAL ENTRY.

L F	Bills Receivable Dr....................	100	00	
L F	To S. H. Blake			100	00

Transactions Involving Shipments and Consignments.

Shipments.—When a person has goods which he cannot dispose of to advantage at home, he may send them to some one doing business in another city or town, and by this means may find a better market.

These transactions give rise to shipments and consignments.

Shipment is the fictitious name given to Mdse. or other personal property sent by you to be sold on your account and risk. You apply this name to the transaction in order that you may know what a certain kind of Mdse. costs and produces you.

It is debited when the goods are shipped for their cost to you, and for all they cost in shipment.

It is credited by its net proceeds when the Account Sales is received by making the person to whom the goods are shipped, or whatever he has remitted you in payment, Dr. to the shipment.

Consignments.—Goods that are received to be sold on commission or on the account and risk of other parties, and for which you retain a certain percentage as your commission, are known as "Consignments."

Consignments should be numbered consecutively, as follows:—Smith's Cons'g't. No. 1; Jones' Cons'g't. No. 1; Smith's Cons'g't. No. 2, or Smith's Cons'g't. A., Smith's Cons'g't. B.

Consignments are debited when received, to all costs or charges paid by you.

Consignments are debited when you render an ac. sales, to the net proceeds if remitted at the time, if not, credit the Consignor.

They are credited with all sales.

The net proceeds should balance the account.

You are generally allowed a commission on the selling price of the goods—1, 2, 3 or 5% being the average allowance.

Insurance is frequently charged on goods for the time they are warehoused.

First Study—*(Shipments).*

Example 37. Adam shipped Ben, Toronto, Ont., to be sold on his acc. and risk 250 bbls. Flour @ $4.25, paying charges in cash $15.00.

Example 37.—ADAM'S ENTRY.

L F	Shipment to Ben No. 1 Dr....		1077	50
L F	To Mdse..........................		1062	50
L F	" Cash.....		15	00

Example 38. Adam receives intelligence from Ben that part of the goods have been sold and he forwards cash $600.00.

EXAMPLE 38.—ADAM'S ENTRY.

L F	Cash Dr............................	600	00		
L F	To Shipment to Ben No. 1....			600	00

Example 39. Adam receives a letter stating that the balance of the goods have been damaged to the extent of 25% of their invoice price.

NOTE.—He simply makes a memorandum of the fact. It is certainly a loss and the loss will be shown by the closing entry. If he wishes to close his books before receiving an account sales this loss must be entered after which he closes the account By Balance Inventory.

Example 40. Adam received an acct. sales as follows :—Total sales, $1010 ; Total charges, $45 ; Net Proceeds, $965. to his credit.

EXAMPLE 40.—ADAM'S JOURNAL ENTRY.

L F	Ben Dr.............................	965	00		
L F	To Shipt. to Ben No. 1.			965	00

Example 41. Adam receives a check for the amount shown to be due him per acct. sales.

EXAMPLE 41.—ADAM'S ENTRY IN CASH BOOK.

L F	Cash Dr............................	965	00		
L F	To Ben..............................			965	00

SECOND STUDY—(*Consignments*).

Example 42. George receives from James to be sold on commission 950 bbls. Potatoes @ $1.25. Paid freight on same per check $20.00.

EXAMPLE 42.—GEORGE'S JOURNAL ENTRY.

James' Con. No. 1 Dr................	20	00		
To Bank...........			20	00

Example 43. George sells 200 bbls @ $1.50 to J. Jones for cash $100 and note at 60 days for balance.

EXAMPLE 43.—GEORGE'S JOURNAL ENTRY.

Cash Dr...............................	100|00	
Bills Rec. Dr............................	200|00	
To James' Con. No. 1.............		300|00

Example 44. He pays insurance $5.00 in cash, and cooperage, per check, $4.00.

EXAMPLE 44.—GEORGE'S JOURNAL ENTRY.

James' Con. No. 1 Dr................	9|00	
To Cash............................		5|00
" Bank............................		4|00

Example 45. He renders an account—Sales—charging 3% commission for selling; $10 storage, and remitting cash $100 and Jones' note at 60 days.

James' Con. Dr......................	271|00	
To Commission....................		9|00
" Storage.......................		10|00
" Cash..........................		52|00
" Bills Rec......................		200|00

Example 46. He sells balance of potatoes for $900, Cash.

EXAMPLE 46.—GEORGE'S ENTRY IN C. B.

Cash Dr...........................	900|00	
To Jones' Con. No. 1.............		900|00

4—PARTNERSHIP BUSINESS.

Most of the commerce of the world is carried on by communities or companies of men These may be either large or small—if large they are generally known as corporations, if small consisting of two or more individuals, they are called partnerships.

A corporation holds its charter. A partnership is conducted according to the terms of its agreement and may be composed of twenty members or under. The capital is paid in by the members of the firm according to the terms of the agreement. The partners' accounts may be adjusted in the following ways:

Invest equal sums and share equal profits and losses

Invest unequal sums and share equally.

Invest unequal sums and share according to investment.

One invest money the other time and experience each sharing equally.

Both giving equal time, ability and experience but contributing unequal sums. Let the one having the lesser capital pay interest to the other on one half the difference between their investments and then share gains and losses equally.

Where two or more invest the capital and one of them manages the business the manager should be paid a fair salary for his work and then the balance of the gains,. if any, shared according to investment.

Partnership is very trying to all interested and should not be entered upon without the greatest consideration and care. Each one's disposition, habits, political, religious and business opinions should be weighed and unless a previous acquaintance has shown that the parties have every reason to look for a continued mutual confidence, better not enter.

Partnerships may be formed by persons of sound mind not under age or legal disability. They may choose to be (a) active, (b) silent or domant,[1] (c) nominal (d) special.

Partnerships may be desolved by,
  (a) Mutual consent of the parties.
  (b) Death or insanity of any one.

(c) The expiration of the contracted period.
(d) The completion of the work agreed upon.
(e) Request of any one of the parties if the time was not specified.
(f) Bankruptcy of one or of the firm.

PARTNERS' CAPITAL ACCOUNT.

Dr.	Cr.
Charge each partner with his liabilities assumed by the firm on beginning business, what he withdraws for his private use and his net loss (if any) at the time of settlement.	Credit each partner by his investment on beginning business, by each subsequent investment (if any) and by his net gain (if any) at the time of settlement.

PARTNERS' PRIVATE ACCOUNT.

Dr.	Cr.
Charge this a/c with all sums taken out for private use.	This a/c closes into Partners' capital account.

Partnership Settlement is an adjustment of Partners' accounts setting forth the net investment, liabilities assumed, withdrawals, gains or losses, and showing their net capital or net insolvency at closing or settling the partnership interests. The bases of partnership adjustments are the articles of co-partnership or contract between the parties.

Settlements are made :
(1) On admitting a new member to the firm.
(2) On dissolving partnership.
(3) At regular intervals as agreed.

Gains and losses are divided:
(1) By precentage.
(2) By fractions.
(3) By proportion.

TRANSACTIONS INVOLVING PARTNERSHIP SETTLEMENTS.

Example 47. Smith and Jones form a co-partnership, agreeing to share gains and losses, in the Brokerage business, according to investments. Smith puts in $10,000, and Jones puts in $15,000.

EXAMPLE 47.—JOURNAL ENTRY.

Cash Dr..........................	25000|00	
To Smith......................		10000|00
" Jones.......................		15000|00

Example 48. The total net gain resulting from the above co-partnership during the first period is $1500. Make the proper Journal entry.

EXAMPLE 48.—JOURNAL ENTRY.

Loss and Gain Dr................	1500 00	
To Smith......................		600 00
" Jones......................		900 00

Example 49. J. Swinton and J. Dunn form a partnership, with Dunn as special partner; Dunn to share ¼ gain and losses and to receive $3 weekly as salary. Swinton's resources:—Cash, $500; Mdse., $2820.75; personal a/c. Inventory, $44.48; Expense Inventory, $200; Fixtures Inventory, $275. Swinton's Liabilities:—Note favor D. Johnston, $175; owes B. Scott on acc. $50. Dunn's investment: $300 Cash.

EXAMPLE 49.—JOURNAL ENTRY.

(a) Cash Dr.	800 00	
Mdse. Dr. 2820.75+44.48......	2865 23	
Expense Dr....................	200 00	
Fixtures Dr...................	275 00	
To Swinton................		3840 23
" Dunn...................		300 00
(b) Swinton Dr..................	225 00	
To Bills Pay...............		175 00
" B. Scott...		50 00

Example 50. J. Jones, S. Evans and W. Smith have this day, Nov. 1st, began business under the style and firm name of Jones, Evans & Co., Gains and Losses to be divided according to investment. Jones invests a deposit in Bank of Toronto, $7000. Evans invests a deposit in the Bank of Toronto,

$6000. Smith invests Cash, $2500; Mdse., $4500; J. Stevenson's note at 3 mos., dated Aug. 15th, 1888, bearing interest at 7% face of note $1000. J. H. Secord owes Smith $350.

EXAMPLE 51.—JOURNAL ENTRY.

Bank of Toronto Dr.............	13000	00	
Cash Dr.........................	2500	00	
Mdse. Dr........................	4500	00	
Bills Rec. Dr...................	1000	00	
Interest Rec. Dr................	14	50	
J. H. Secord Dr.................	350	00	
To Jones.....................			7000 00
" Evans......................			6000 00
" Smith......................			8364 58

Example 51. Divide a net gain of $126 among the above named partners in the proportion of 7, 6 and 8, making the proper Journal entry to show the accounts affected.

EXAMPLE 51.—JOURNAL ENTRY.

Jones Dr......................	42 00	
Evans Dr......................	36 00	
Smith Dr......................	48 00	
To Loss and Gain.............		126 00

Example 52. Journalize: Evans withdrew for private use, Mdse. $15, Cash $10.

EXERCISE 52.—JOURNAL ENTRY.

Evans Dr......................		
To Cash....		10 00
" Mdse....................		15 00

Example 53. A, B and C are partners, having invested $1010.50, $2000 and $2995 respectively. They gained $600 during the first half year. Make a Journal entry shewing each one's a/c properly credited. (Divide in proportions 1, 2, 3 their investments are so very nearly equal to these ratios.)

EXAMPLE 53.—JOURNAL ENTRY.

Cash Dr.....................	600|00	
To A....		100|00
" B........................		200|00
" C........................		300|00

Example 54. James and John are equal partners in a $10,000 concern, and it has been agreed that should either increase or decrease his capital during the year he should be charged or allowed interest at the rate of 6% per annum ; and the gains and losses shared equally. Accordingly we find (a) James withdrew $1000 at the end of 4 mos., and (b) John invested $1000 at the end of 4 mos. Make a Journal entry adjusting their accounts at the close of the year.

EXAMPLE 54.—JOURNAL ENTRY.

James Dr.........................	1100|00	
To John.........................		1100|00

Example 55. A and B engage in business March 1st, 1889, each investing $1600; June 1, A increased his investment $400, and B drew out $300. Make the necessary Journal entries and an adjusting entry March 1st, 1890.

EXAMPLE 55.—JOURNAL ENTRY.

1889. March......	1	(a)	Cash Dr.....	3200|00	
			To A........................		1600|00
			" B........................		1600|00
June.,.......	1	(b)	Cash Dr........................	400|00	
			To A..........		400|00
June........	1	(c)	B Dr..........	300|00	
			To Cash.....................		300|00
1890. March......	1	(d)	B Dr.....................	13|50	
			Interest Dr...................	4|50	
			To A.....................		18|00

Example 56. C and D, who were to share gains and losses, C ⅔, D ⅓, have lost $360 during the year. Make a Journal entry shewing the proper debits and credits.

EXAMPLE 56.—JOURNAL ENTRY.

C Dr..............................	240|00	
D Dr..............................	120|00	
To Loss and Gain..............		360|00

JOINT STOCK COMPANY TRANSACTIONS.

As to the question of dividend :—As soon as the amount of the dividend is known this is next converted into so much per cent. on the stock, paid in. It is seldom that a company declares a dividend to the full extent of the earnings of the year. They usually declare an even dividend. Example :--If the company has earned 12½ per cent. they would likely declare a dividend of, say 10 per. cent. What is left would remain at the credit of loss and gain, or it might be carried to the credit of "Undivided Profits" or "Rest Account" or "Surplus Account." The effect this "Rest" account has on the stock and standing of the company is to enhance it. Besides this the "Surplus" account may be taken, that is a portion of it, any year that the company does not net the usual dividend, thus keeping up a uniform income for those dependent upon it for their sustenance. In years of general depression when failures occur in rapid and serious succession, the possession of a "Rest" account enables the company to meet all obligations and still declare the customary dividend. Another advantage in possessing a "Rest" account is that it prevents undue fluctuation resulting from varying dividend.

When the dividend is declared we debit loss and gain and credit dividend No. 1 or No. 2, as the case may be.

When the dividend has been paid to the shareholders debit dividend and credit cash.

Example 57. A company which had a net profit for the year of $20,000 upon a capital of $200,000, declares a dividend of 6% per annum : 2% going to Rest a/c and 2% is paid in stock.

EXAMPLE 57.—JOURNAL ENTRY.

L F	Profit & Loss Dr.	$20,000|00		
L F	To Dividend No. 1.		$12,000	00
L F	" Rest		4,000	00
L F	" Capital Stock.		4,000	00

Example 58. You bought 24 shares of Tallapoosa (Georgia) L. M. & M. Co'ys Stock at $20.00 each, and sold them at $30.00 each the same evening.

EXAMPLE 58.—JOURNAL ENTRY.

Cash Dr.	$240|00	
To Loss & Gain.		$240|00

Example 59. Instead of selling immediately you keep your stock for some time and finally sell as in example No. 58.

EXAMPLE 59.—JOURNAL ENTRY.

(a)	T. L. M & M. Co'ys Stock Dr.	480|00	
	To Cash		480|00
(b)	Cash Dr.	720|00	
	To T.L.M. & M. Co'ys Stock. ...		480|00
	" Loss & Gain.		240|00

Example 60. You bought 20 shares Ontario Bank Stock @ par value $100 each. Some time later you sell 10 shares at 15% premium. Cash received therefor being $1150.

EXAMPLE 60.—JOURNAL ENTRY.

(a)	Ont. Bank Stock Dr.	2000|00	
	To Cash		2000|00
	Cash Dr.	1150|00	
	To O. B. Stock.		1000|00
	" Loss & Gain.		150|00

Example 61. At the close of a year there is to the credit of Profit & Loss a/c of a certain company, $5,000 as their net profit. Pay $2,000 in dividends, place $2,000 in Rest a/c, and let the balance remain at the credit of Profit & Loss.

EXAMPLE 61.—ADAM'S ENTRY.

(a)	Profit & Loss Dr....	4000	00	
	To Dividend			2000 00
	" Rest.....			2000 00

Example 62. You have succeeded in placing 20 year 4% Local Improvement Debentures for the City of Ottawa to the amount of $30,000, at a premium of 3⅓%.

EXAMPLE 62.—JOURNAL ENTRY.

	Cash Dr.....................	31,000	00	
	To Debentures..........			30,000 00
	" Profit & Loss.................			1000 00

DISCOUNTING AND RENEWING NOTES AND DRAFTS.

Example 63. Discounted at La Banque Nationale, Wm. Smith's note. Face $200. Discount $2.00; Proceeds to my credit.

EXAMPLE 63.—JOURNAL ENTRY.

	La Banque Dr.......	198	00	
	Discount "	2	00	
	To Bills Receivable................			200 00

NOTE.—If Cash had been received for proceeds, Cash instead of Banque would have been the Debit.

Example 64. Discounted at La Banque Nationale, Wm. Smith's note due 3 mos. hence @ 6₀/° from the present. Face $300. Proceeds received in cash $295.50.

EXAMPLE 64.—JOURNAL ENTRY.

	Cash Dr...........................	295	50	
	Discount..........................	4	50	
	To Bills Rec......			300 00

Example 65. Prepaid my note favor J. Jones, in cash. Face $25. Discount allowed off $2.50.

EXAMPLE 65.—JOURNAL ENTRY.

L F	Bills Pay Dr..	25	00		
L F	To Cash			22	50
L F	To Discount....			2	50

NOTE.—If check had been given in settlement of above, Banque would have been the credit instead of Cash.

Example 66. James Mack's note matured yesterday which I had previously discounted, at Ontario Bank, and was protested for non-payment. To-day I took it up by check. Face $40. Protest charges $1.35.

EXAMPLE 66.—JOURNAL ENTRY.

L F	Protested Paper, Dr......	41	35		
L F	To Bank			41	35

Example 67. If the above had not been discounted but remained in my possession, and I had had it protested, give my entry, paying fees in cash.

EXAMPLE 67.—JOURNAL ENTRY.

L F	Protested Paper Dr.	41	35		
L F	To Bills Rec			40	00
L F	Cash Dr......................			1	35

Example 68. Drew on S. Evans at 10 days to balance a/c $400, and immediately discounted same at La Banque.

EXAMPLE 68.—JOURNAL ENTRY.

L F	La Banque, Dr......................	398	25		
L F	Discount "	1	75		
L F	To S. Evans...................			400	00

Example 69. Instead of Discounting I remit above draft to Wm. Good on a/c.

EXAMPLE 69.—JOURNAL ENTRY.

L F	Wm. Good, Dr.................	400	00		
L F	To S. Evans...................			400	00

Example 70. After discounting above draft as in Example, I hear through the Bank that he would not accept, but remits $300 and a note at 3 mos. for balance, which note I have placed to my credit.

NOTE.—The Banque should not charge anything for placing above note to your credit, as they have already charged you sufficient to carry small note of 100, 3 mos—so that no entry would be required.

Example 71. Wm. White renews his note in my possession and favor for 2 mos. Face of old note $200. Face of new note $202. Interest being at $6°/_o$.

EXAMPLE 71.—JOURNAL ENTRY.

L F	Bills Rec., Dr.................	202	00		
L F	To Discount			2	00
L F	" Bills Rec...................			200	00

Example 72. William King has made an assignment offering 75c in the dollar, which I accept. I hold a note against him for $750, and he pays me in cash.

EXAMPLE 72.—JOURNAL ENTRY.

L F	Cash Dr........................	562	50		
L F	Loss & Gain Dr................	187	50		
L F	To Bills Rec...................			750	00

5.—DAY BOOK TRANSACTIONS TO BE JOURNALIZED.

1. Sold Jones & Co., Montreal, Mdse. amounting to $500. Received payment in full per ck. on Bk. of Montreal.. $500
2. My Aunt having left me a legacy of $10,000, I invest the amount in business. $10,000
3. Discounted Smith & Thomson's note of the 16th ult. for $1000, at the Bk of Commerce. Discount off 60 days @ $6°/_o$.

4. Sold J. Hammell Mdse to the amount of $125.50.
    Recd. in payment Cash 25.50, Note @ 60 days for bal.
5. Invested in business Cash $500, Mdse $600, Real Estate
    $400 .... $1500
6. Sold T. Graham, Mdse $300. Recd in payment ck on
    Ontario Bank.
7. Bot of Jas. Oliver & Son, Mdse. amt'g to $800. Gave in
    payment ck. on Bk of Ottawa.
8. Bot of Smith, Brown & Co., on my note @ 10 days, Mdse
    amounting to.................................... $350
9. Rec'd of Blackburn & Mason, N.Y., to be sold on their
    account and risk, Mdse $1250, charges prepaid.
10. Shipped Jackson & Stewart, Quebec, to be sold on my
    acct. and risk, Mdse invoiced to them at.......... $680
11. Recd of S. Stewart & Son, Montreal, to be sold on their
    account and risk, Mdse $1000. Paid freight, etc., in cash $10
12. Sold P. Flinn from Blackburn & Mason's consgt. for cash,
    Mdse amt'g to.................................. $100
13. The goods sold from Blackburn & Mason's Consgm't. to
    P. Flinn, having been damaged in transportation owing
    to imperfect packing, we have remitted him cash allow-
    ance $25
14. Rec'd from Jackson & Stewart, Quebec, an "acct. sales"
    of Mdse shp'd them the 10th inst., Net proceeds re-
    mitted in cash. $700
15. Deposited in Bk of Ottawa, Cash.................. $1,000
16.   PROMISSORY NOTE.
    $600.00.   Ottawa, Oct. 4th, '89.
    Thirty days after date I promise to pay to J. Finney or order, ($600) Six hundred
Dollars, for value received.
                                            G. THOMPSON.
    (a) Give Thompson's journal entry. (b) Give Finney's journal
entry upon receipt of above note.

17.   RECEIPT ON ACCOUNT.
    $25.50.   Ottawa, Oct. 4th, 1889.
    Rec'd of Thos. Black on a/c ($25.50) Twenty-five Dollars and Fifty cents.
                                            SAMUEL SKIGGS.
    (a) Give Samuel Skiggs journal entry.

18.   RECEIPT IN FULL.

Ottawa, Oct. 4th, '89.
Rec'd of Chas. Blackwell, Cash in full of acct.

GEO. WHITE.

(*a*) Give Chas. Blackwell's journal entry.

19.   RECEIPT FOR RENT.

Ottawa, Oct. 4th, '89.
Rec'd of A. Snyder, Cash for one month's rent from date, of house No. 68 Blank St.

J. ATKINS.

(*a*) Give J. Atkins' journal entry.

20.   ACCEPTANCE.

$50.00.   New York, Oct. 1, 1889.
Thirty days after date pay to J. Jones, or order, Fifty Dollars and charge the same to my acct.
T. W. Currier, Esq.,
   Ottawa, Ont.

WM. CONNOR.

(*a*) Give Currier's journal entry ; (*b*) J. Jones ; (*c*) Wm. Connor.

21.   DRAFT.

$25.00.   Ottawa, Oct. 4, '89.
F. Hyman, Montreal.
At one day's sight pay to Geo. Munro, or order, Twenty-five Dollars, and charge the same to acct. of

R. LOVELL.

(*a*) Give R. Lovell's journal entry.

22.   DUE BILLS.

$78.00.   Ottawa, Oct. 4th, 1889.
Due W. G. Thomas, Seventy-eight Dollars, on demand.

W. G. EVANS.

(*a*) Give W. G. Evans' entry ; (*b*) W. G. Thomas' entry.

23.   I. O. U.

$10.00.   Ottawa, Oct. 4th, '89
T. Allen. I.O.U. Ten Dollars.

S. FARMER.

(*a*) Give T. Allen's entry.

24.   CHATTEL NOTE.

Ottawa, Oct. 4th, 1889.
One year after date for value received, I promise to pay G. W. Graham, or order, One Hundred Dollars in Spring Wheat, good and merchantable at ruling prices.

W. C. CLARKINS.

(*a*) Clarkins' entry ; (*b*) Graham's entry.

25. Bot of Durham & Co., Montreal, Mdse to the amt. of $750. Gave in payment J. Jones' note of the 20th ult. for $825, receiving cash balance $70.00. Discount allowed off note $5.00.

26. I have this day taken as partner into the business H. Everly, who invests to the amt. of $5000.00—½ cash, ½ Mdse.

27. An order is a request from one man to another directing him to pay to a third party a certain sum of money mentioned in the order. (a) If A gives B an order on C for $10 worth of goods, what entry would C make ?

28. The difference between an order and a draft is : In the order one man requests another to pay cash or goods, limiting or not limiting the amount ; but in the draft he requests him to pay unconditionally, a certain sum of money in a specified time. (a) If M draws on N at one month for $20.00 in his own favor, what entry does M make?

29. A promissory note is one which is payable in cash, while a chattel note is one which is payable in goods or any personal property other than money.

(a) Contrast the necessary journal entries made in each case by the payee of a Promissory and a Chattel Note.

30. In a joint note, all who sign it promise to pay their share ; but in a joint and several note each takes the responsibility of paying the whole or a part of it.

31. Negotiable paper is paper that can be transferred from one to another for a consideration or otherwise; while non-negotiable paper is only of value to the person in whose favor it is made.

32. The resources and liabilities of student and W. J. Green upon beginning business to-day, No. 4 Sparks St. Student invests cash $2675 and he owes Brouse Bros., L'Orignal, Ont., on a/c $175. W. J. Green invests cash $2500.

33. Paid cash for office fixtures $75, for office stationary $10.

34. Deposited in the Bank of Ottawa $4500.

35. Leased store of C. W. Bangs and paid him one month's rent of store in advance $60, by check on Bank of Ottawa.

36. Borrowed cash of J. M. Musgrove $250 at 3 °/₀ interest

37. Bought of Russell, Seybold & Co. per Invoice, No 1, goods valued at $3000, and gave check or Bank of Ottawa in payment.
38. Sold James Gibson, on a/c, merchandise amounting to $50.50.
39. Paid Brouse Bros., on a/c $100 cash.
40. Bought of J. Macdonald, Toronto, goods per Invoice amounting to $276, gave in payment note at 10 days payable at Bank of Ottawa, here.
41. Bought of E. Robinson & Co. merchandise amounting to $100 per Invoice, on 30 days.
42. Paid freight on goods from J. Macdonald in cash $10.
43. Bought sight draft on Montreal at ¼ °/, exchange at Bank of Ottawa for $200 by check and remitted to Brouse Bros., L'Original, to apply on account.
44. Bought of Sinclair, Jack & Co., Montreal, merchandise valued at $256.
45. Sold J. Hope & Co. 100 reams unruled foolscap paper, sent to us by mistake, from Montreal, invoiced at $3.25 a ream.
46. Gave Sinclair, Jack & Co., your note dated to-day at 3 days, payable at Bank of Ottawa, to apply on account, $300.
47. Deposited in Bank of Ottawa, cash, $150.
48. Received of J. Hope & Co,, City, their note, to apply on account, dated to-day, at one month, payable at Bank of Ottawa, with interest $325.
49. Advertised in Citizen, Free Press and Journal for book-keeper, paid for same in cash, $3.
50. Bought draft on Montreal at ¼ °/, exchange at Bank of Ottawa by check, for amount due Sinclair, Jack & Co. Remitted same.
51. Received cash of James Gibson, on a/c, to the ½ his indebtedness.
52. Gave J. Macdonald check on Bank of Ottawa, to apply on a/c $50.
53. Discounted at Bank of Ottawa J. Hope & Co's. note and had the proceeds placed to our credit.
54. Gave Sinclair, Jack & Co. your check on Bank of Ottawa, to balance account.
55. Received, cash, $200 of J. Hope & Co. to apply on their note which you had discounted.

56. Paid clerks salaries in full $75.
57. Deposited in Bank of Ottawa, cash, $100.
58. Bought of Blakeman & Co., New York, silks per invoice, $750, gave in payment draft at 10 days sight.
59. Sold W. H. Lang, H. W. Kilbe and James G. Blaine a bill of merchandise amounting to $900, for which each one becomes responsible for ⅓.
60. Received cash of James Gibson to balance account.
61. Exchange checks with Harris & Campbell for their accommodation, gave them your check on Bank of Ottawa, dated to-day, and received from them their check on Bank of Montreal, dated to-morrow, each for $262.20.
62. Received of J. Hope & Co. $50 to apply on their note which you hold.
63. Received of W. H. Lang his note at 30 days payable at Bank of British North America, to apply on account $75.
64. Bought of Blakemam & Co., New York, summer silks per Invoice amounting to $316, gave in payment sight draft for $116 which we purchased at Bank of Ottawa at ¼ °/₀ exchange, giving check in payment, also sent them our promissory note at three months, to balance account.
65. Deposited in the Bank of Ottawa all the cash on hand.

MODEL DAY-BOOK.

SET I.—PRIMARY.

(6)   PORT HOPE, Ont., June 1st, 1889.

		$	c.	$	c.
*√	Bannell Sawyer begins business, investiig Cash..	840	00	840	00
	——————3——————				
√	Bot. for Cash, 25 bbls. Flour @...............	4 25	106 25	106	25
	——————4——————				
√	Sold C. Clemes & Son for Cash, 10 bbls. Flour @	5 10	51 00	51	00
	——————5——————				
√	Bot. of D. J. McLennan, for Cash, 60 bbls of Flour @......	4 40	264 00	264	00
	——————7——————				
√	Sold J. M. Hawkins, on his aceeptance at three days, 50 bbls. Flour @......	5 60	280 00	280	00
	——————8——————				
√	Sold John Mitchell, for Cash, 25 bbls. Flour @..	5 70	142 50	142	50
	——————9——————				
√	Bot. for Cash, 20 bbls. Flour @........	4 30	86 00	86	00
	——————10——————				
√	Sold Geo. Glass & Co., for Cash, 15 bbls. Flour @	5 00	75 00	75	00
	——————11——————				
√	Sold J. M. Hawkins, on his note at 10 days, 5 bbls. Flour @............	4 90	24 50	24	50
	——————12——————				
√	Rec'd Cash for J. M. Hawkins' acceptance of the 7th inst...............................			280	00
	——————14——————				
√	Bot. of D. J. McLennan, on our note at 30 days, 6 bbls. Flour @.......................	4 80	28 80	28	80
	——————15——————				
√	Paid sundry expenses in Cash...................			24	00
	——————16——————				
√	Sold for Cash, 6 bbls. Flour @................	5 00	30 00	30	00
				$2232	05

ACCOUNTS to be opened in the Ledger in this Set are as follows:—Bannell Sawyer, allowing 4 lines; Cash, 8 liues; Flour, 8 Lines; Bills Receivable, 4 lines; Bills Payable, 2 lines; Expense, 2 lines; Loss and Gain, 4 lines; Balance, 4 lines.

* This check mark shows that the entry before which it is placed has been transferred to the Journal.

MODEL JOURNAL.
SET 1.—PRIMARY.
(9)   Port Hope, Ont., June 1st, 1889.

REASONS FOR DEBITING AND CREDITING.	L.F.	JOURNAL ENTRY.	$	c.	$	c.
C. is debited because received into the business. B. S. is credited because he put the money into the business.	(2) (1)	Cash Dr.......... To B. Sawyer Cr.	840	00	840	00
		—3—				
F. debited because received. C. credited because parted with	(3) (2)	Flour Dr......... To Cash Cr.	106	25	106	25
		—4—				
C. C. & Co. not mentioned because they pay for what they get	(2) (3)	Cash Dr......... To Flour Cr.	51	00	51	00
		—5—				
D. J. McL. not mentioned in Journal entry because you paid him in full.	(3) (2)	Flour Dr......... To Cash Cr.	264	00	264	00
		—7—				
B. R. debited because a promissory note or draft (i.e. a bill), has been received, and for which in 3 + 3 = 6 days you expect payment	(5) (3)	Bills Rec. Dr..... To Flour Cr.	280	00	280	00
		—8—				
J. M's name does not appear in Journal entry because he paid you in full for what he got and should not now be debited or credited.	(2) (3)	Cash Dr......... To Flour Cr.	142	50	142	50
		—9—				
F. debited because received, C. credited because paid out.	(3) (2)	Flour Dr......... To Cash Cr.	86	00	86	00
		—10—				
Reasons as in No. 8.	(2) (3)	Cash Dr......... To Flour Cr.	75	00	75	00
		—11—				
B. R. debited because another's promise to pay is received, and for which bill we will receive payment	(5) (3)	Bills Rec. Dr..... To Flour Cr.	24	50	24	50
		—12—				
B. R. credited because it has been "paid," "given out" or "parted with."	(2) (5)	Cash Dr......... To Bills Rec. Dr.	280	00	280	00
		—14—				
B. P. debited because our promise to pay (bill payable), has been given out—parted with.	(3) (4)	Flour Dr......... To Bills Pay. Cr.	28	80	28	80
		—15—				
Expense is debited because it has cost us value.	(6) (2)	Expense Dr...... To Cash Cr.	24	00	24	00
		—16—				
Same as in No. 4.	(2) (3)	Cash Dr......... To Flour Cr.	30	00	30	00
			$2232	05	$2232	05

Note.—The student will copy Journal given above, omitting "Reasons" to the left, as he has no space in his book for giving the reasons, but he should study so as to be able to apply them in subsequent work.

MODEL LEDGER—SET I., PRIMARY.

(1)

Dr.   (Liabilities & Losses.)   BANNELL SAWYER.   (Resources & Gains.)   Cr.

June	16	To Balance (R. Ink)	L 8	933	95	June	1	By Cash	9	840 00
						"	16	" Loss and Gain ..	L 7	93 95
				933	95					933 95

(2)

Dr.   (Receipts.)   CASH.   (Paid Out.)   Cr.

June	1	To Bannell Sawyer..	9	840	00	June	3	By Flour..........	9	106 25
"	4	" Flour, ...	9	51	00	"	5	" "	9	264 00
"	8	" "	9	142	50	"	9	" "	9	66 00
"	10	" "	9	75	00	"	15	" Expense.........	9	24 00
"	12	" B. Rec.........	9	280	00	"	16	" Balance (R. Ink).	L 8	938 25
"	16	" Flour.	9	30	00					
				1418	50					1418 50

(3)

Dr.   (Cost of Purchases).   FLOUR.   (Proceeds from Sales).   Cr.

June	3	To Cash	9	106	25	June	4	By Cash	9	$ 51 00
"	5	" "	9	264	00	"	7	" B. Rec..........	9	280 00
"	9	" "	9	86	00	"	8	" Cash	9	142 50
"	14	" B. Pay.........	9	28	80	"	10	" "	9	75 00
"	16	" Loss&Gain(R.Ik)	L 7	117	95	"	11	" B. Rec..........	9	24 50
						"	16	" Cash	9	30 00
				603	00					603 00

(4)

Dr   (Our Notes Redeemed)   BILLS PAYABLE.   (Our Notes Issued).   Cr.

June	16	To Balance (R. Ink)	L 8	28	80	June	14	By Flour..........	9	28 80

(5)

Dr.   (Others' Notes Rec'd).   BILLS RECEIVABLE.   (Others' Notes Red'd).   Cr.

June	7	To Flour..........	9	280	00	June	12	By Cash	9	280 00
"	11	" "	9	24	50	"	16	" Balance (R. Ink)	L 8	24 50
				304	50					304 50

(6)

Dr.   (Cost)   EXPENSE.   (Closing.)   Cr.

| June | 15 | To Cash | ...... | 9 | $ 24 | 00 | June | 16 | By Loss & Gain (R. Ik) | L 7 | $24 | 00 |

(7)

Dr.   (Losses).   LOSS AND GAIN.   (Gains).   Cr.

June	16	To Expense......	L 6	$24	00	June	16	By Flour........	L 3	$117	95
		" B. Sawyer (R.Ik)	L 6	93	95						
				$117	95					$117	95

(8)

Dr.   (Resources).   BALANCE.   (Liabilities).   Cr.

June	16	To Cash	L 2	$938	25	June	16	By Bills Payable ...	L 4	$ 28	0
"	"	" Bills Rec......	L 3	24	50	"	"	" Bannell Sawyer .	L 1	933	95
				$962	75					$962	75

SET I.—TRIAL BALANCE

No.	LEDGER TITLES.	L.F.	Dr.		Cr.	
1	Bannell Sawyer......................	3	$		$ 840	00
2	Cash..............................	3	1418	50	480	25
3	Flour.............................	3	485	05	603	00
4	Bills Receivable	4	304	50	280	00
5	Bills Payable.......................	4			28	80
6	Expense	3	24	00		
			$2232	05	$2232	05

STATEMENT OF LOSS AND GAIN.

No.		L F	Loss.		Gain.	
3	Flour, difference, a gain	3	$		$117	95
6	Expenses, debit a loss	6	24	00		
	Difference, B. Sawyer's *net gain*	6	93	95		
			$117	95	$117	95

6.—RESULTS.

ABOUT TRIAL BALANCES.

Statements and *Balance Sheet*,—their various forms and what they show.

When your posting is completed, the Ledger should have equal debits and credits. This does not mean that each account must have equal debits and credits (that would be absurd) but that the sum of the debits of the accounts in the Ledger must equal the sum of the credits of the accounts in the Ledger. To know this you should take off a "trial balance." It is taken as follows:—Rule a form similar to a page of the Journal and enter the titles of all accounts found in the Ledger, then beginning with the first account add up the debit side putting down the amount below the account and into the Trial Balance (debit column) in ink. Do the same with the credit side and so on with other accounts. Add up the sums on each side of Trial Balance and if the total debit is equal to the total credit the work is presumed to be correct, if they are not equal you should proceed to find and correct the error, as follows :

1. See that the columns of the Trial Balance have been correctly added.

2. See that the accounts in the Ledger have been footed up correctly.

3. See if the footings have been correctly transferred from the Ledger to the Trial Balance.

4. See if the columns of the Journal have been correctly added.

5. See that each entry has been correctly posted, checking (in this way √) each amount both in the Ledger and the Journal.

5. See if any amount stands in the Ledger without a check mark √) opposite it, if any, search for the cause of it.

ERRORS IN TRIAL BALANCES.

The trial balance is not *positive* evidence of the correctness of a Ledger; at the same time no Ledger can be correct without the trial balance footings are even. If they are not even the cause is likely on account of having omitted an entry, posting to the wrong account or transferring wrong accounts. If an error certainly exists then ascertain its *exact amount*, and then look carefully for the same amount in the Journal, which may have been omitted in posting.

TRIAL BALANCE "A".

NOTE.—This T. B. shews the balance of each acct. in the Ledger from which it has been taken. The Dr. is kept on the left and the Cr. on the right as in the Ledger. By Mdse there has been a gain of $200, and by Expense there has been a loss of $100. Thus shewing a net result of $100, which is a *net gain*. This *net gain* ($100) added to the *net investment* ($1800) equals the *present worth* ($1900). The accounts are numbered to the left, and the pages on which the accts. may be found in the Ledger are kept to the right.

Dr. Balance.	No.	Ledger Titles.	L F	Cr. Balance.
	1	Stock, net Investment........	1	1800
600	2	Cash on hand.............	1	
	3	Mdse., gain.	2	200
1000	4	Bills Rec., other's notes on hand..	3	
600	5	J. Jones, he owes me..........	4	
	6	S. Evans, he owes me..........	5	300
100	7	Expense, cost of business, a loss..	8	
2300				2300

2nd TRIAL BALANCE "A".

NOTE.—After transferring all the differences of the accts. to Loss & Gain, and Balance, a T. B. of Stock, L. & G., and Balance accts. is often taken, as follows:—

	Ledger Titles.	L F	Dr. Figs.	Cr. Figs.
1	Stock................	1	200 00	1662 50
2	Loss and Gain...............	9	182 50	20 00
3	Balance	9	1300 00	
			1682 50	1682 50

TRIAL BALANCE "B".

NOTE.—This T. B. will shew the same results as T. B. "A". The figures to the right and left shew the sums of the different accts. in the Ledger. To find the balances of the accts. subtract the footings.

DR. Figs.	NO.	LEDGER TITLES.	L.F	CR. Figs.
200	1	Stock....................	1	2000
1200	2	Cash.....................	1	600
1400	3	Mdse.....................	2	1600
1300	4	Bills Rec.................	3	300
1600	5	J. Jones.................	4	1000
200	6	S. Evans.................	5	500
100	7	Expense..................	8	
6000				6000

2nd TRIAL BALANCE "B".

NOTE.—The same result as in 2nd T. B. "A" may be shewn by taking the differences instead of the footings, as here shewn.

		LEDGER TITLES.	L F	DR. BAL.	CR. BAL.
	1	Stock......................	1		1462 50
	2	Loss and Gain.............	9	162 50	
	3	Balance....................	9	1300	
				1462 50	1462 50

TRIAL BALANCE "C".

NOTE.—This is the same as T. B. "A", shewing the same results, but the Dr. and Cr. balances are side by side to the right. A more convenient arrangement than in T. B's "A" and "B".

No.	Ledger Titles.	L F.	Balances.	
			Dr.	Cr.
1	Stock........................	1		1800
2	Cash.........................	1	600	
3	Mdse	2		200
4	Bills Rec.....................	3	1000	
5	J. Jones......................	4	600	
6	S. Evans.....................	5		300
7	Expense......................	8	100	
			2300	2300

TRIAL BALANCE "D."

NOTE.—Gives same results as previous T. B's, but the *footings* are kept to the right.

	Ledger Titles.		Dr. Figs.	Cr. Figs.
1	Stock........................	1	200	2000
2	Cash.........................	1	1200	600
3	Mdse.........................	2	1400	1600
4	Bills Rec.....................	3	1300	300
5	J. Jones......................	4	1600	1000
6	S. Evans.....................	5	200	500
7	Expense......................	8	100	
			6000	6000

TRIAL BALANCE "E".

NOTE.—Gives same results but shews both footings and balances.

DR. Figs.	DR. B.	No.	LEDGER TITLES.	L F	CR. Figs.	CR. B.
200		1	Stock....................	1	2000	1800
1200	600	2	Cash	1	600	
1400		3	Mdse	2	1600	200
1300	1000	4	Bills Rec.................	3	300	
1600	600	5	J. Jones..................	4	1000	
200		6	S. Evans.................	5	500	300
100	100	7	Expense.................	8		
6000	2300				6000	2300

TRIAL BALANCE "F".

NOTE.—Gives same results, but shews both footings and balances to the right in most convenient situation, where they may be readily contrasted.

No.	LEDGER TITLES.	L F	DR. Figs.	DR. Bal.	CR. Figs.	CR. Bal.
1	Stock	1	200		2000	1800
2	Cash.	2	1200	600	600	
3	Mdse......	3	1400		1600	200
4	Bills Rec.	4	1300	1000	300	
5	J. Jones	5	1600	600	1000	
6	S. Evans.	6	200		500	300
7	Expense......	7	100	100		
			6000	2300	6000	2300

HOW TO LOCATE ERRORS IN TRIAL BALANCES.

1. See that your T. B. has been carefully added.
2. Test the footings of the accounts in the Ledger.
3. See that these footings have been correctly transferred.
4. See that the Journal balances.
5. If the error be 1, 10, 100, 1000, etc., it is likely an error in adding.
6. If the error is divisible by 2 it is likely caused by posting an item to the wrong side of an account
7. If divisible by 9 it likely occured by interchanging the figures, *i.e.* 241 for 214 or 496 for 946, and so on. The differences 27 and 450 are each divisible by 9. And so other numbers.
8. The last resort is to see that the posting is correct, checking each entry by each book from which posting has been done.
9. A good plan is to check over the posting before taking a trial balance.
10. The habit of *care* both in posting and adding cannot be too strictly enjoined. Nine-tenths of all student's errors consist in errors of addition and carelessness in posting.

TRIAL BALANCE.

No.	Names of Accounts in Ledger	L.F.	Dr. Footings.	Cr. Footings
1	Stock, (Capital or Proprietor)	1		1000
2	Cash.............................	1	2000	1200
3	Mdse.	2	1600	1800
*4	Bills Receivable	2	300	200
5	Bills Payable..........	2	100	500
6	B. M. Tally.......................	3	600	100
7	Expense.........................	3	200	
			4800	4800

(a) What do the figures to the left of the names represent?

(b) What do the figures in the column marked L. F. represent?

(c) What do the Dr. and Cr. footings of the Trial Balance shew?

(d) How often should a Trial Balance be taken off in business?

(e) What different names are given to the proprietor's account?

(f) When do you debit Stock, Mdse, B. Pay, and Expense, and when do you credit them?

(g) What was the proprietor "worth" on beginning business?

(h) On which occount has he gained: on which has he lost?

(i) What amount of Mdse., did he purchase? How much cash did he disburse? What amount of his own note (Bills Payable) has he issued? Does any one owe him on account? If so, how much?

(j) What did it cost him to carry on his business during the term?

TRIAL BALANCE

No.	Names of Accounts in Ledger	L. F.	Inventory	Dr. Footgs.	Cr. Footgs
1	D. T Ames (Proprietor).......	4		200	2800
2	Cash..................	4		4000	3500
3	Merchandise....	4	4500	12 000	9500
4	Bills Receivable	5		4300	320
5	Bills Payable............. . .	5		6400	8200
6	Hughes & Co................	6		520	640
7	Ostrom & Ostrom	7		1500	1600
8	T. Bradburn.................	9		1200	2450
9	Expense.....................	12	720	1380	
10	Interest & Discount	12		420	30
			5220	31,920	31,920

(a) Classify the above accounts into Fixed and Fluctuating.

(b) What was Ames' "net worth" on beginning business?

(c) What has been his net gain or loss since?

(d) What is he now worth?
(e) Find the sum of his liabilities and of his resources.
(f) What is an Inventory?
(g) How can expenses account have an Inventory?
(h) Why is the greater amount on the credit side of B. Pay?
(i) Could Expense account have the credit side the larger?
(j) What does T. Bradburn & Co's a/c shew? (1) the debit side, (2) the credit, (3) the balance.

TRIAL BALANCE.

No.	Names of Accounts in Ledger	L.F.	Inventory	Dr. Footgs.	Cr. Footgs.
1	George S. Bean } (Partners)	1		200	2000
2	J. J. Rooney... }	1		300	2100
3	Cash..........................	1		9600	8500
4	Mdse.........................	2	3500	5600	3500
5	Bills Receivable.............	4		1400	1000
6	Bills Payable................	5		8000	14,600
7	Real Estate..................	6	2400	2000	
8	E. B. Stone..................	6		1460	260
9	W. J. Moore..................	7		3000	
10	Expense......................	9	60	360	
11	Interest.....................	10		230	190
			5,960	32,150	32,150

(a) Classify the accounts into Fixed and Fluctuating.
(b) What was the "net worth" of each partner at commencement.
(c) What was the "net worth" of the firm?
(d) Find the firms "net gain" or loss since?
(e) How much of this will each one share?
(f) What is the "present worth" of each partner?
(g) What is the "present worth" of the firm?

TRIAL BALANCE.

No.	Names of Accounts in Ledger.	L F	Dr. Balces.	Cr. Balces.
1	Cash..............................	1	4000	
2	Mdse	1		1075
3	John Roberts	2	500	
4	Robert Black	2	200	
5	S. Evans...........................	3		975
6	D Smiley...........................	4		2725
7	Bills Payable	4		100
8	Expense......	5	175	
			4875	4875

(a) Suppose you began business one year ago *without* capital and that your books now exhibit the above balances, what has been your gain?
(b) What amount do you owe?
(c) What is your net worth?
(d) What monthly salary have you earned?
(e) Which amounts shew your gains and losses?
(f) Give the journal entry you would make if you were beginning business now and were assuming the obligations, etc., indicated above, though you open your own books.

TRIAL BALANCE.

No.	Names of Accounts in Ledger.	L F	Dr Balces	Cr. Balces.
1	Mdse.	1		1720
2	William Smith	2		15000
3	James Edwards	2	7750	
4	Cash................................	3	4270	
5	Bills Receivable................	3	5050	
6	Bills Payable...........	3		500
7	Expense.	4	150	
			17220	17220

(a) Shew that the "net gain" resulting from the business is seen from above T.B. to be $1570.

PERSONAL ACCOUNTS RECEIVABLE.

No.		Dr.	Cr.	Balance.
1	L. A. Edgerton...............	2675 00	2500 00	175 00
2	W. W. Harkness.............	1259 77	550 00	709 77
3	J. B. Forde.....	2150 00	1650 00	500 00
4	H. W Harding	603 26	357 87	245 39
		6688 03	5057 87	1630 16

PERSONAL ACCOUNTS PAYABLE.

No.		Dr.	Cr.	Balance.
1	Crouse Bros................ .	634 72	834 72	200 00
2	Geo. H. Smith.............	1122 33	1321 50	199 17
3	Judson & Co.............	384 00	485 50	100 50
4	Ham & Forbes	873 26	1273 26	400 00
5	Perrin & Reed..............	1037 56	1357 67	320 11
6	Lawrence & Co.............	1244 48	2720 25	1475 77
7	Beekman, Bros.	1357 03	1688 89	331 86
8	Scott, Bar & Son.	944 89	1094 17	149 28
9	E. Robinson............ ...	425 25	748 81	323 56
		8023 52	11,524 77	3500 25

A Balance Sheet should show as follows :—

1. Name of *Firm*.
2. No. of accounts.
3. Date when taken.
4. Ledger Titles.
5. Ledger Folio.
6. Debit and Credit footings.
7. Inventory.
8. Loss & Gain Statement.
9. Stock or Partners' Accounts.
10. Assets and Liabilities.

STUDENTS' BALANCE SHEET, TAKEN OCT. 1st, 1889.

OTTAWA, *Oct. 1/89.*

	L F	Trial Balance Dr.	Trial Balance Cr.	Inventory	Cost Accounts Loss	Cost Accounts Gain	Stock Dr.	Stock Cr.	Financial Position Resources	Financial Position Liabilities
1 Stock	1	200	2000				200	2000		
2 Cash	1	1200	600						600	
3 Mdse	2	1400	1600	750|42		950|42			750|42	
4 Bills Rec	3	1300	300						1000	
5 J. Jones	4	1600	1000						600	
6 S. Evans	5	200	500							300
7 Expense	8	100			100					
		6000	6000	750	42	850	42	950	42	2650	42	2850	42	2950	42	
					950	42		2850	42		2950	42	

(R.I.) Stock's Net Gain...... 950|42

(R.I.) Stock's Net Worth...... 2850|42

7.—EXERCISES IN POSTING.

NOTE:—Open the necessary Ledger accounts and post the following items to their respective places. Do not open a Journal, the entries are easy and should be Journalized mentally. For form of Ledger see Model Set, pages 63 and 64.

1890.   FIRST STUDY.

Jany. 1st   G. S. Bean began business with cash on hand....$1900 00
           J. Jones owes him on a/c, (included in investment),   350 00
   2   Bot. of A. Hall, for cash, goods valued at.......   70 00
      Bot. of S. Evans, on a/c, Mdse. for use in store...   25 00
      Bot of T. Dolan & Co., on ac., 1 suit clothes for self.   30 00
      Bot of Stetham & Co., for cash 2 door locks @ $1.   2 00
   3   Sold J. Hawley, on a/c., 10 yds tweed @ 90c....   9 00
      Sold J.W. Brisbin, for note at 10 days, goods....   12 00
   4   Paid for office lamp........................ ....   5 00
      Paid clerk, on a/c., of salary..................   3 00
   5   Paid rent in advance, 1 month.................   20 00
   6   Recd. of J. Hawley, on a/c. cash...............   5 00
   7   Paid for local advertising......................   2 00
   8   Paid for letterheads and envelopes.............   7 00
   9   Paid T. Dolan & Co. on a/c....................   20 00
  10   Paid for 1 load of wood for store 4 00
      Deposited in Ontario Bank.................... 1000 00

ACCOUNTS to be used: G. S. Bean (Proprietor) Cash, Mdse., Bills Receivable. S. Evans, T. Dolan & Co., J. Hawley, Ontario Bank, Expense Advertising, Loss and Gain.

(1) Show the net loss or gain. (2) Show amount of personal accounts receivable.

SECOND STUDY.

1890.
Feby 1st   J. J. Rooney began boot and shoe business investing Cash $1,000.00 and Mdse. $500.00.
       Rented store on Water St. at $300.00 per. annum payable monthly in advance.
       He pays one month rent in cash..............$ 25 00
       Bot. store fixtures, for cash.....................   75 00
       Bot. office stationery, for cash.................   15 00
       Bot an assortment of goods of J. Carey on 3 mos. a/c 450 00

2   Signed advertising contracts with
             Examiner $120.00
             Review $120.00
             Times $120.00
       for ¼ col. space in daily and weekly edition of each paper for one year at figures set opposite. Space to be paid for monthly in equal installments.

NOTE:—Debit Advertising and credit Bills Payable, for the reason that whether your space is occupied or not you will be called upon for payment as promptly as though a promissory note had be n given in each case.

3   Sold A Robinson, Jr., on a/c goods worth 100 00
4   Bot. of Foote & McWhinney, on a/c, 2 cases mens' slippers 50 00
    Paid Examiner, Review and Times one month's advertising in advance 20 00

NOTE:—Debit B. Pay. and Credit Cash.

5   Sold M. H. McWilliams, Madoc, on 10 days' a/c 1 case rubbers 20 00
6   Paid for letter press for office use 7 00
7   Appropriated for private use, cash 12 00
8   Paid railway fare to Port Hope, and sundry other expense items to Lindsay and Norwood, while engaged in distributing circulars, etc 5 00
9   Recd. 10 cases goods from W. J. Wise & Co., Toronto, for which we have sent them our note at 10 days 300 00
10 Paid freight on above goods in cash 5 00

NOTE:—Debit Mdse.

    Sold A. Robinson, goods, per. invoice 25 00
    Recd. in payment an order on Foote & McWhinney

ACCOUNTS to be used. J. J. Rooney, (Proprietor), Cash, Mdse. Bills Payable. J. Carey, A. Robinson, Jr., Foote & McWhinney, M. H. McWilliams; Expense, Advertising, Fixtures, Loss and Gain.

(1) Show J. J. Rooney's present worth, supposing $1000 worth of Mdse. remains unsold. (2) Providing the stock of mdse. and fixtures had been burned.

1890   THIRD STUDY.

March 1. Student began business to-day investing cash $1500.
     2. Bot of E. H. Turner, Peterboro, for cash 100 pairs Men's Kipp Boots @ $3.00.
     3. Sold W. H. Stevens, Peterboro, on a/c, 50 pairs American Rubbers @ 40c.
     4. Sold A. L. Davis, Toronto, for cash, 60 pairs ladies' Slippers @ 1.25.
     5. Recd. cash of W. H. Stevens to apply on a/c, $10
     6. Bot of C. Doney, Ottawa, on 30 days a/c, 2 cases, 200 pairs, ladies' F. C. Boots @ $2.00
     8. Bot of Brown, Edmondson & Co., for cash, 1 case, 100 pairs Kid Shoes @ $1.50
   12. Sold J. Pratt & Co., on a/c, ½ case, 50 pairs Ladies' F. C. Boots @ $3.00
   15. Sold E. B. Edwards, Peterboro, on a/c, ½ case, 50 pairs, Kidd shoes @ $2.
   17. Bot of M. C. Baines, N. Y., on a/c, 2 cases, 200 pairs Am. Rubbers @ 25c.
   20. Sold, for cash, ½ case Ladies' F. C. Boots @ $3.00.
   24. Sold M. H. Stevens, Pbro., on a/c, 1 case, 100 pairs Am. Rubbers @ 40c.
   25. Recd. of E. B. Edwards, on a/c, cash $50.
   26. Sold, for cash, ½ case Am. Rubbers @ 40c.
   30. Bot, at auction sale, goods valued at $500. Paid Cash.
   "   Paid M. C. Baines, on a/c, $40.

INVENTORY : Mdse. unsold $700. (a) Find the net gain. (b) Tell the total sales.

1890   FOURTH STUDY.

April 1. Student invests in stationery business cash........$2500 00
        Personal a/c receivable (per P. L.)............... 5000 00
     2. Bot of Jones & Co., Montreal, for note at 30 days,
        Mdse. per Invoice...... .... 125 00
     4. Sold A. L. Davis, Peterboro, on note at 20 days,
        Goods, per S. B......................... 375 00
     5. Received of W. H. Stevens, his note at 30 days in
        full of a/c................................ 900 00

6	Paid H. C. Jennings, Brantford, in full of a/c......	2500	00
7	Cash sales to-day.............................	75	00
8	Sold James Graham on a/c, per S. B.............	687	50
10	Bot of Pratt & Co., for cash, per Invoice.........	200	00
11	Recd. Cash of James Graham, on a/c, per S. B...	1000	00
12	A. L. Davis paid his note of 4th inst., in cash......	375	00
15	Sold James Graham, on a/c, Mdse. per S. B.......	650	00
17	W. H. Stevens paid his note of 5th instant, to-day, in cash...................................	900	00
19	Paid our note of 2nd, instant, favor Jones & Co., in cash...........	125	00
21	Sold James Hope & Co., on their note at 10 days, Mdse, per S. B........................	331	25
25	Bot of Durie & Son, on 30 days note, goods per In.	575	00
30	Unsold goods destroyed by fire.		

(a) Find loss. (b) Find total purchases. (c) Find sum of liabilities, (d) Find cash in hand.

QUESTIONS

ON WORK COVERED BY EXAMINATION ON NOTES AND DRAFTS.

See pages 36, 37, 40 and 41.

What is a promissory note? What is a draft? What is the maker? the payee? What do you mean by maturity? What are the essentials of a promissory note? Write out a note negotiable by endorsement. What kinds of endorsements are there? Why are endorsements made? What two points may the purchaser of a note be called upon to establish? Why is a note protested? On what kind of bills are days of grace not allowed? Why should an endorsed note be presented for payment on the very day on which it matures? What is a joint note? Distinguish between joint note and joint and several. What is an accommodation note? When does the drawee become a party to a draft? Give the wording of special, general and qualified endorsements. Give the rules for journalizing drafts.

SET II.—PRIMARY.

LINDSAY, Ont., 1st June, 1889.

		$	c.	$	c.
Geo. S. Bean, commenced business to-day with a Capital of:—					
Cash, per C. B.		10000	00		
Mdse. per Inventory		5000	00	15000	00
———2———					
Bot. of Bradburn & Co. for Cash.					
6 Cases, 8460 yds Prints, at	9	761	40		
5 Cases, 4654 yds Ginghams at	12¼	581	75		
1 Case, 250 yds C. Flannel, at	15	37	50	1380	65
———3———					
Paid Cash for Office Stationery, etc.		100	00	100	00
———4———					
Bot. of Dundas & Flavelle, for Cash.					
1340 yds Tricots	51	683	40		
275 yds Broadcloth 2	50	687	50	1370	90
———5———					
Deposited in the Bank of Toronto, Cash at 3 per cent. interest		6000	00	6000	00
———6———					
Sold J. Graham, on acc't.					
400 yds Gingham	15	60	00		
75 yds Broadcloth. 3	00	225	00	285	00
———8———					
Sold G. W. Beall, for Cash.					
940 yds Tricots	70	658	00		
645 yds C. Flannel	34	219	30	877	30
———9———					
Paid Clerk hire		30	00	30	00
———10———					
Sold for Cash, 75 yds Broadcloth 3	50	262	50	262	50
———11———					
Sold John Kennedy, on 60 days' credit.					
400 yds Tricot	72	288	00	288	00
———12———					
Bot. of Bradburn & Co., on acc't.					
10 cases, 14080 yds Prints	8½	1196	80	1196	80
———13———					
Rec. of J. Graham, Cash in full of acc't		285	00	285	00
———14———					
Sold John Kennedy, 5 cases, 7050 yds Prints...	11	775	50	775	50
Rec'd Cash, $275.50; balance on acc't. $500					
———17———					
Sold J. W. Wallace, on his note at 4 mos.					
2 cases, 2873 yds Prints	12	344	76	344	76
———18———					
Paid expenses in cash.		175	05	175	05
———20———					
Paid Bradburn & Co. on acc't		1000	00	1000	00
		$29371	46	$29371	46

(Red Ink) *Inventory:* *Value of unsold Goods, $6822.55.*

SET II.—LEDGER TITLES.—Geo. S. Bean, 4 lines; Cash, 10; Mdse. 9; Bank of Toronto, 2; J. Graham, 2; John Kennedy, 4; Bradburn & Co., 4; Bills Rec., 2; Expense, 5; Loss and Gain, 4; Balance, 7.

SET II.—PRIMARY.

STATEMENT OF LOSSES AND GAINS.

	Losses.	Gains.
Mdse. Dr. or cost............ $8948.35		
" Cr. or proceeds........$2833.06		
" Inventory (goods unsold). 6822.55 9655.61		
" Difference, a gain		707 26
Expense Dr., a loss.............................	305 05	
George S. Bean's net gain (Red Ink)	402 21	
	707 26	707 26

SET III—PRIMARY.

STATEMENT OF RESOURCES AND LIABILITIES.

No.	Accounts with Persons.		Resources	Liabilities
1	Cash Dr. amount received $2669 20			
	" Cr. " paid out................ 1810 53			
	" Difference, a resource (Red ink)......		858 67	
2	Mdse. on hand per Inventory, a resource....		6220 83	
3	B. Rec. Dr. amount of Bills Receivable	1150 50		
	" Cr. " " settled	400 00		
	" Difference, a resource (Red ink)....		750 50	
4	Bills Pay. Cr. amount of Bills issued	2300 00		
	" Dr. " " redeemed....	200 00		
	" Difference, a liability (Red ink) ..			2100 00
5	Geo. A. Cox Dr. amount he owes me......	175 00		
	" Cr. " I owe him	300 00		
	" Difference a liability (Red ink)			125 00
6	P. L & I.Works Co., I owe them, a liability			105 00
	J. J. Rooney's net worth (Red ink)....			5500 00
			7830 00	7830 00

SET III.—PRIMARY.

———— Peterborough, Ont., 1st June, 1889. ————

I. F						
	J. J. Rooney commenced business to-day with the following resources and liabilities :					
	Resources :—					
	Cash, on hand........................			$2000 00		
	Mdse., on hand per Inventory............			3500 00		
	Bills Rec., Jas Kendry's note, due 5th inst..			400 00		
	Adam Hall, owes on a/c.			100 00	6000 00	
	Liabilities.—I owe as follows :					
	Bills Pay, my note due 10th inst., favor Jas. Stevenson......................			200 00		
	Geo. A. Cox, on a/c.....................			300 00	500 00	
	————— 2 —————					
	Bot. of The Gibb W. & I. Co. (Montreal) for Cash.					
	10 Reels of Barb Wire..............10 00			100 00		
	10 Rolls Wire Gauze 15 00			150 00	250 00	
	————— 2 —————					
	Bot. of Pillow, Hersey & Co., Montreal					
	100 bbls Cut Nails...................	3	25	325 00		
	20 " Pressed Nails	4	00	80 00		
	25 Gross Brads....................	1	10	27 50		
	5 Cwt. Railway and Pressed Spikes ..	5	00	25 00		
	10 Gross Horse Shoes 10		00	100 00		
	50 Gross Carriage Bolts, $1.20 ; 50 Gross Tire Bolts			105 00		
	10 Gross Coach Screws	4	20	42 00		
	10 Gross Hot Pressed Nuts..........	1	20	12 00		
	10 Gross Forged Nuts.............	2	30	23 00		
	10 Doz. Felloe Plates....:..	4	10	41 00		
	20 Gross Lining and Saddle Nails.....	2	30	23 00		
	25 Gross Tufting Buttons.............	1	15	28 75		
				832 25		
	Rebate from list prices 12½ per cent. (that is ⅛)			104 03		
					728 22	
	Gave in payment Jas. Kendry's Note, $400, cash for balance, $328.22.					
	————— 6 —————					
	Bot. of McKechnie & Bertram (Dundas, Ont.) for Cash.					
	15 Doz. Punches.....................	1	00	15 00		
	12 Doz. Shears, assorted sizes.........	2	20	26 40	41 40	
	(Red Ink) Carried forward...........				$7519 62	

PETERBOROUGH, Ont., 7th June, 1889.

	$	c.	$	c.
Brought forward........			7519	62
——— 7 ———				
Bot. of W. H. Banfield, (T. ... J, Ont.) for cash.				
10 Knitting Machines, $25	250	00		
10 Sets Tinsmith's Tools, $16.25..........	162	50		
	412	50		
Rebate from list prices................$41.25				
10 per cent. and 5 per cent. off 18.56	59	81		
			352	69
——— 8 ———				
Bot. of Thomas Robertson & Co., Montreal.				
1 car load Pig Iron, 24,365 lbs. 3c..........	730	95		
" Bar Iron, 24,537 lbs. 5c..........	1226	85		
1 Lot (assorted) Steam and Gas Fittings.....	475	25	2433	05
Gave in payment notes at 2 mos., $600; 3 mos., $600, and 4 mos., $800; Cash for balance, $433.05.				
Bot. of the Peterborough Lock and Iron Works.				
50 doz. Door Locks, complete, $4.10	205	00	205	00
Gave in payment draft on self at 30 days, for $100, balance to remain on open acc't.				
——— 9 ———				
Paid sundry items for Freight and Cartage.......	165	17		
Paid Clerk hire...........................	40	00	205	17
Sold R. Kingan & Co., Mdse. per invoice, for Cash	569	20	569	20
Sold M. Miller for note at 30, Mdse. amounting to...	750	50	750	50
——— 10 ———				
Sold Geo A. Cox on acc. Mdse. per invoice......	175	00	175	00
Received from Adam Hall, payment in full of acc't..	100	00	100	00
Paid my note favor Jas Stevenson, due to-day......	200	00	200	00
			12510	23

NOTE.--I want to admit James Stevenson as silent Partner, who will invest cash equal to my net worth. Journalize, post and take off statements—when this is done close all the accounts, bring down all balances, and open an account for James Stevenson, crediting him with his Cash investment This leaves your books ready for business again.

(Red ink) INVENTORY:—Mdse. unsold per books, $6220.83.

SET III.—LEDGER TITLES—J. J. Rooney, 5 lines; Cash, 10; Mdse., 11; Bills Rec., 5; Bills Pay., 5; Adam Hall, 2; Geo. A. Cox, 5; the P. L. & I. Works, 3; Expense, 2; Loss and Gain, 2; Balance, 6.

Sample of C. B. used in Junior Practice.

Dr.   **CASH.**   **Cr.**

1889.		Receipts.				1889.		Disbursements.			
Oct.	1	Student, investmt	1		500	Oct.	1	Fixtures, desk & [books]	5	30	
"	2	Mdse., sales	3		100	"	"	Expense, circ'l'rs	5	15	
"	3	Jones, on a/c....	4		25	"	"	Mdse., Inv. No. 1	3	200	245
"	4	B. Rec., Young's [note	4		400	"	6	Balance, on hand	2		790
"	"	Interest on above	4	10	535						
					1035						1035
Oct.	7	Balance	2		790						

Note.—In working the Junior Sets the C. B. should be kept as above illustrated. The balance is carried down to the left, ready for next day's business, and when posting put nothing in Cash account in the Ledger except the *balance* on hand.

Sample of J.-D. B. used in Junior Practice.
JOURNAL DAY-BOOK.
Peterbrro, Ont., 1st Jan'y, 1889.

	Journal Entry. D.-B. Entry Abbreviated.	Dr.	Cr.
* ✓	Cash Dr	500	
	Mdse. Dr .... per Stock book	200	
	B. Rec. Dr....... J., 's' note due 26th inst..	150	
	J. Thoms Dr....... he owes on acc...........	150	
	To Stock. .... J. Smith's investment.......		1000
	William Dr ...... 20 yds. Twee. at 1.00.......	20	
	To Mdse.		20
	Expense D .... Cartage acc..............	5	
	To C. Cook................................		5
		1025	1025

Note.—This form of book should be used by the student hereafter; being convenient and compact. * This check mark is to shew that cash must not be posted. Cash should be posted from the C. B. only, and then only the *balances*.

8.—JUNIOR PRACTICE.

DIRECTIONS.

Your attention is first called to your capital of $500.00, which is given you for the purpose of conducting a general store in Peterborough.

The commission for selling goods for others will be 3 %.

Fold and file all business papers, except Bills Payable and Bill Receivable, according to the following :—1st, the name of the paper ; 2nd, the name of the firm from which it has been received ; 3rd, the date to the left hand ; 4th, the amount to the right hand under the firm name.

Filings should be written in a small neat style, having red ink ruling underneath.

All Bills of "Mdse," Invoices and Acc't Sales should receive your initials and the word "Ex."

WORKING RULES.

1.—The work of each set must be examined by the principal.

2.—Errors must be corrected before the work of the next set is begun.

3.—A trial balance will be required with each set and a balance sheet with the last.

4.—Your Bank Book must be handed in for balancing at the end of each set.

5.—Cash Ac. must agree with the cash on hand.

6.—Accept no currency that is disfigured or torn.

SET FIRST.

Books used :—Day Book, Journal, Ledger, Cash Book, Check Book.

TRANSACTIONS.

Place, Peterborough.

1.—Invest cash, $500.

2.—Buy your supply of goods from some wholesale house.

3.—Buy and sell for cash 6 times, recording the transaction each time in your Day Book, using any name that may be convenient.
4.—Buy and sell 5 times on a/c.
5.—Deposit what cash you have in the College Bank.
6.—Buy and sell 6 times giving and receiving checks in payment.
7.—Journalize.
8.—Post.
9.—Take off Trial Balance.
10.—Close Ledger and present books for examination.

SET SECOND.

TRANSACTIONS.

Place, Ottawa.

1.—State your Resources and Liabilities, resulting from first set.
2.—Buy and sell on a/c three times.
3.—Buy and sell for note 3 times
4.—Buy mdse., not less than $150. Give in payment, check one-half, note at 60 days for balance.
5.—Sell mdse., not less than $100, receiving in payment check, cash and note @ 30 days each, ¼ balance on a/c.
6.—Receive a consignment of mdse. to be sold on a/c and risk of consignor, not less than $230.
7.—Sell for cash half of No. 6, making $25.
8.—Deposit in College Bank cash on hand.
9.—Sell remainder of consignment at cost on 30 days a/c.
10.—Journalize. Post. Take off Trial Balance.
11.—Close Ledger and present books for examination.

SET THIRD.

TRANSACTIONS.

Place, Toronto.

1.—Lease Store No.... Hunter Street, at $360 per annum, payable monthly.
2.—State your financial position resulting from Second Set.
3.—After posting your Resources and Liabilities, take off Trial Balance—if correct, proceed.
4.—Buy mdse. not less than $100. Give in payment cash for one-half, check for balance.

5.—Deposit in College Bank any cash you may have in your possession.
6.—Buy and sell 6 times, payment in various ways.
7.—Buy mdse. not less than $150, giving joint and several note.
8.—Receive a consignment.
9.—Sell consignment at an advance of 10 per cent.
10.—Ren'd Ac. Sales. Com. 3 per cent. on sales. Storage 1 per cent. of value.
11.—Sell all your mdse. by auction.
12.—Journalize and Post, close and show result on Balance Sheet.
13.—Collect all outstanding ac's, pay all debts.
14.—Present work for examination.
15.—Return any Currency or Blanks you may have to the Principal.

LETTERS.

1—REQUESTING PAYMENT OF AN ACCOUNT.

Peterboro, Ont., March 16th, 1889.

J. K. Boy, Esq.,
    Ottawa, Ont.

DEAR SIR :—The balance of your account, ($25) twenty-five dollars, is considerably over due, and I write to call your attention to the matter. Our expenditures at present are such that we must request the prompt settlement of all over due accounts.

                Yours very truly,
                    BANNELL SAWYER.

NOTE :—Care must be taken not to give offence when requesting payment of an ac. Most men are honest either from pride or moral principle and they will square accounts in time, if not insulted or compelled.

2—REPLY APPOLOGIZING FOR DELAY AND ENCLOSING THE AMOUNT.

Ottawa, March 20th, 1889

MR. BANNELL SAWYER,
    Peterboro, Ont.

DEAR SIR :—Your letter of the 16th inst. to hand and I have to apologize for my tardiness in remitting. Enclosed please find P. O.

Order for ($25) twenty-five dollars to balance account. Please send receipt in full by early mail and oblige,

Yours respectfully,

J. K. Boy.

NOTE:—The receipt asked for in this letter should be forwarded without delay and kept for at least 6 years by the recipient.

3—ANOTHER REPLY TO NO. 1, THE ACCOUNT HAVING BEEN SETTLED AND A RECEIPT HELD.

Ottawa, March 20th, 1889.

MR. BANNELL SAWYER,
  Peterboro, Ont.

DEAR SIR :— Your letter of the 16th, inst., to hand calling attention to a balance of an overdue account. There must be some error or omission in your accounts for I hold a receipt dated Feb. 28th in full of account.

Yours respectifully,

J. K. Boy.

NOTE:—You observe how useful the receipt may here become.

4—CALLING ATTENTION TO AN ERROR IN INVOICE RECEIVED.

Ottawa, Ont., April 4th, 1889.

W. J. GAGE & Co.,
  Toronto, Ont.

GENTLEMEN :—On checking over the Invoice of goods received from you a few days ago, I find an overcharge of ($14) fourteen dollars. Kindly credit my account with this amount and remit "credit slip."

Yours respectfully,

BANNELL SAWYER.

NOTE—A "credit slip" is usually an "account form" printed in red and filled in crediting a person who had been previously overcharged. The recipient should attach it to the Invoice containing the overcharge.

5—ANSWER TO NO. 4 STATING THE ERROR HAS BEEN CORRECTED.

Toronto, Ont., April 6th, 1889.

MR. BANNELL SAWYER,
  Ottawa, Ont.

DEAR SIR :—Your letter of the 4th, inst., calling our attention to an over charge of ($14) fourteen dollars, has been received. We are sorry the mistake was made and have credited your account with amount of error per inclosed "credit slip."

Yours very truly,

W. J. GAGE & Co.

6—ANSWER TO NO. 4 STATING THAT THE AMOUNT IS RIGHT, BUT, THAT AN ITEM HAS BEEN OMMITED IN COPYING FROM SALES BOOK.

Toronto, Ont., April 6th, 1889.
Mr. BANNELL SAWYER,
Peterboro, Ont.

DEAR SIR :—Your letter of the 4th, instant, calling our attention to an over charge of ($14) fourteen dollars, has been received. On referring to our Sales Book we find that the amount of Invoice rendered is correct and the seeming overcharge is accounted for by our having omitted entering 7 doz. handkerchiefs @ $2 = $14. Doubtless by this time you have found that they were not named in the Invoice.

Yours respectfully,
W. J. GAGE & Co.

NOTE:—Before reporting errors business men should very carefully check over each item in a consignment of goods with the Invoice, then verify the extensions and additions, thus avoiding unnecessary correspondence.

7—A REQUEST FOR A CREDIT OF $1000 GIVING REFERENCES.

Peterboro, Ont., April 12th, 1889.
JNO. MACDONALD & CO.,
Toronto, Ont.

GENTLEMEN :—Finding my capital insufficient to meet the wants of my customers, I write to ask you for a credit of $1000, for three months. For any information you may desire I am premitted to refer you to Messrs W. J. Gage & Co., of your city, and to Wm. Smith of this place. Awaiting the favor of an early reply.

Very respectfully yours,
FRED J. PRATT.

NOTE:—The danger in a letter of this kind is that the merchant will get too anxious for credit and by using too many adjectives, loose his chances of accommodation. The object in giving a reference residing in same city as your correspondent is to expedite the shipment of goods.

8—MACDONALD WRITES TO WM. SMITH FOR INFORMATION RESPECTING F. J. PRATT'S RELIABILITY.

Toronto, Ont., 15th April, 1889.
WM. SMITH,
Peterboro, Ont.

DEAR SIR:—Fred. J. Pratt of your town has asked us for a credit of $1000, for three months, referring to you. Kindly let us know by early mail whether we would be safe in complying with his request and oblige,

Yours respectfully,
JNO. MACDONALD & CO.

9—SMITH'S REPLY.

Peterboro, Ont., 16th April, 1889.
JNO. MACDONALD & CO.
Toronto, Ont.

GENTLEMEN:—Yours of the 15th, inst., inquiring of the responsibility of Fred. J. Pratt, of this town, received. In reply I have pleasure in saying that he is known to be honest and reliable.

Yours truly,
WM SMITH.

NOTE :—You will please notice the absence of gossip in this letter and the straight forward statement made, "known to be honest and reliable."

10—A REFERER'S UNFAVORABLE REPLY TO ENQUIRIES.

Ottawa, Ont., 16th April, 1889.
JNO. JOHNSTON & CO.
Toronto, Ont.

GENTLEMEN :—Yours of the 15th, instant inquiring of the responsibility of W. J. Wilkins, of this city, received. In reply I must say that it is rather doubtful whether you would be safe in giving him credit or not. He has lately made improvements on his premises and incurred other expenditures which I am satisfied the volume of business done by him does not warrant.

Yours truly
ALBERT HALL.

NOTE :—How soon business men detect a man's weakness or looseness in expenditure? Always keep your expenses down to the lowest limit.

11.—REPORTING INSOLVENCY TO PRINCIPAL CREDITOR.

Ottawa, Ont., 5th April, 1889.
JAMES WALKER & SON.,
Toronto, Ont.,

GENTLEMEN :—I have just finished "stock taking" and find from my "balance sheet" that I am insolvent, happily my assets will realize considerably over 60°/₀ of my liabilities. I will notify all my creditors presently but as you are the one most concerned, I write to you first. My books are open for inspection.

Yours faithfully,
D. W. DAWSON.

NOTE:—The principal creditor very often becomes the assignee. It is always an evidence of honesty to have books in readiness for examination by creditors at any time.

12.—ORDERING BOOKS BY MAIL.

Peterboro, 5th April, 1889.
MESSRS D. APPLETON & SON.,
N. Y. City.

GENTLEMEN :—For the enclosed amount, ($7.50) seven dollars and fifty cents, please send, per American Express, the books named in enclosed list and oblige,

Yours respectfully,
ALBERT STRATON.

NOTE!—Always order on a sheet of paper separate from that on which your letter is written.

13.—THEIR REPLY, THE ORDER HAVING BEEN FILLED.

295 Broadway, N. Y. City, 7th April 1889.
ALBERT STRATON, ESQ.,
Peterboro, Ont.

DEAR SIR :—Your esteemed order, for books, has been received and placed in rotation on our mailing list. You will doubtless receive them by early train. Thanking you for the favor of your valued order, we remain,

Yours truly,
D. APPLETON & SON.

NOTE:—The prompt filling of an order is always an indication of method, and without method no business of any considerable dimensions can be organized.

14—THEIR REPLY, THE ORDER HAVING BEEN PARTIALLY FILLED.

295 Broadway, N. Y. City, 7th April, 1889.
ALBERT STRATON ESQ.,
Peterboro, Ont.

DEAR SIR :—Your valued order for books has been received. We have executed the same with the exception of the Dictionary. This we shall send you in the course of a week, unless advised otherwise.

Yours very truly,
D. APPLETON & SON.

NOTE:—The reason for the insertion of the last words "unless advised otherwise,"—to induce an immediate cancelling of the order for dictionary should the delay prevent the sale.

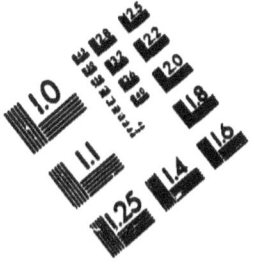 

**IMAGE EVALUATION
TEST TARGET (MT-3)**

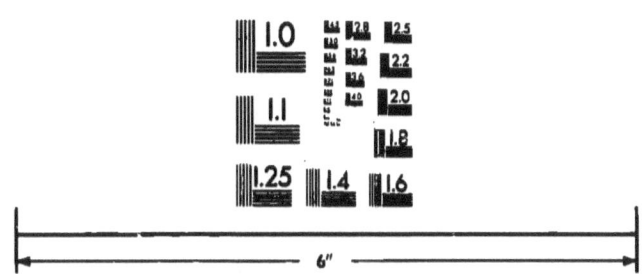

Photographic
Sciences
Corporation

23 WEST MAIN STREET
WEBSTER, N.Y. 14580
(716) 872-4503

15.—DRAWING ON A DEBTOR FOR AMOUNT OF OVERDUE ACCOUNT.

Peterboro, Ont., 15th Oct., 1889.

MR. JAMES EVANS,
    Norwood, Ont.

DEAR SIR :—Your account which is past due, has attracted my attention. It is not customary with us to allow accounts to run past maturity and we have drawn on you through Merchants' Bank, for amount of your account ($51.75.) We trust that you will duly honor the same on presentation.

            Very truly yours,
                RUFUS STEVENSON.

16.—REQUESTING PRICE LIST.

Ottawa, Ont., 17th Oct. 1889.

JOHN MATHEWS, ESQ.,
    Toronto, Ont.

DEAR SIR :—Kindly send us your latest price list.

            Respectfully yours,
                DONALDSON & THOMPSON.

17.—REPLY INCLOSING SAME.

Toronto, Ont., Oct. 19, 1889.

DONALDSON & THOMPSON,
    Ottawa, Ont.

DEAR SIR :—Agreeably to your request, of yesterday, we inclose price list. Shall be pleased to receive your commands.

            Yours truly,
                JOHN MATHEWS.

NOTE.—Many men do one half the trade they might do, on account of their procrastination in filling mail and other orders.

18.—WRITE, ORDERING GOODS OF A FIRM FIRST TIME.

Peterboro, 17th Oct., 1889.

JOHN MATHEWS, ESQ.
    Toronto, Ont.

DEAR SIR :—Please send per Merchants' Express, goods named below, selected from price list received to-day. Draw on us at sight and refer to A. B. of your city.

            Very respectfully yours,
                DONALDSON & THOMPSON.

NOTE:—Reference to A, B. is made so as to establish your credit without delaying the shipment of goods.

19.—APPLICATION FOR AN AGENCY.

Port Hope, Ont., 17th Oct., 1889.

JAS. SHAW, ESQ.
Toronto, Ont.

DEAR SIR :—Your advertisement in to-day's Mail calling for applications for agents has come to my notice and I hereby respectfully offer my services. I have had experience with the following firms to whom I am premitted to refer : Robertson & Son, Whitby ; Garrettson & Son, Guelph ; Rose, Belford & Co., Toronto, Ontario ; and a graduate of a first class Business College. Should you grant me an agency I shall be pleased to enter upon my duties immediately.

Very respectfully yours,

HARRY OKE.

NOTE.—It is unnecessary, in writing a letter similar to above, to give your historys to urge your claims. Never tell out the pathos of your business life. Let the heavens alone hear the story of your failures. Men have neither the time to listen nor the sympathy to aid.

20.—INCLOSING SUBSCRIPTION TO A PAPER.

Port Hope, Ont., April 1st, 1889.

PUBLISHERS "TRIBUNE,"
N. Y. City.

GENTLEMEN :—Inclosed please find seven dollars, being subscription to your paper, the Daily Tribune, for the year ending April 25th, 1890.

Respectfully yours,

S. E. K. WALKER.

21.—CIRCULAR LETTER TO THE PUBLIC ON BEGINNING BUSINESS.

Ottawa, Ont., 1st April, 1889.

DEAR SIR :—I take pleasure in announcing that I have opened a dry goods store at No. 420 Sparks Street, next door to Fairweather & Co's Fur store. I have had some experience with the best houses in this line of trade, and having selected my stock with care I hope to be able to please all intending customers with the quality and freshness of the goods, and the lowness of the prices. My stock of spring goods which will be opened on May 1st inst., is most complete and comprises many novelties for the coming season. Awaiting the pleasure of seeing you early. I remain, Sir,

Yours respectfully,

W. H. CONNOR.
420 Sparks St.

22—COMMISSION MERCHANT SOLICITING CONSIGNMENTS.

Ottawa, Ont., March 6th, 1889.
JAS S. KING,
　　Picton, Ont.

DEAR SIR :—We desire to call your attention to our facilities for placing large consignments of fruit before the trade in this district with the utmost care and despatch. We have been for sometime engaged in the business and have established an excellent business connection. We handle all hardy fruits on a commission of 3%. Quick returns may be anticipated. Hoping to hear from you at your first convenience. We remain,

　　　　　　　　　　　　Yours respectfully,
　　　　　　　　　　　　　BANNELL SAWYER.

The student should study the above sample letters, carefully reading the *notes* subjoined, and then write at least one each week of the following letters, etc., and place on Principal's desk. Letters must be well written on writing paper, enclosed in sealed envelope and properly addressed, giving initials of writer on the envelope in lower left corner.

23.—Write a telegram not exceeding 10 words, ordering 6 pcs. Canadian Tweed of John Macdonald, Toronto, telling him to draw on you at 30 days.

24.—Write telegram to Ottawa, before opening of Parliament, engaging rooms at the Russell.

25.—Cablegram to Liverpool, advising Messrs. Charring, Reed, Clare & Co., of your shipment to them of 500 beef cattle, in charge of S. Evans.

26.—Write a letter to Smith, Elliot & Co., Toronto, asking credit for Wm. Jones, Lindsay.

27.—Write a letter of Introduction and Credit.

28.—Write, answering an advertisement for Book-keeper.

29.—Application for position as Traveller, in answer to advertisement.

30.—Write a recommendation of a general nature for a young mam.

31.—Apology for breaking a business engagement.

42.—Write a letter giving some advice to a young man about to enter business.

NOTE :—For instructions respecting the form, arrangement, parts, etc., of letters see "Studies." page 60.

REMARKS
— ON —
RETAIL SET 1.
BUSINESS, ADVERSE—SINGLE PROPRIETOR.

Special-Cash Book, Journal and Ledger are used as principal books; and B.B. and Personal Ledger as auxiliary.

The Order Book is usually kept lying on the counter, and entries made as they occur. In the evening those that remain unpaid are entered in the Personal Ledger.

The Personal Ledger contains accounts with customers only, and is an auxiliary book. Sales on ac. are regarded as merchandise on hand until the accounts are paid, when Mdse is credited. The ordinary Journal ruling is preferable for a Personal Ledger of this character, because it affords more space for items. All statements of accounts may be made out from the Personal Ledger without referring to any other book.

Take off a Trial Balance at the end of the week, close the loss and gain accounts and bring down Inventories.

Accounts remaining unpaid in the Personal Ledger must be added to the Merchandise Inventory.

Keep no bank ac. in the Ledger. Keep no Cash account in the Ledger: but to get your Trial Balance you must enter the balance of Cash on the debit side of it. The C. B. balance will show all cash in Bank and on hand. Credit cash when a check is given; make no entry for deposits except on stub of Check Book.

The C. B. will have an extra, or a special column on the credit side for "Expense," the total of which may be posted weekly or monthly to the Debit of Expense. Also an extra column on debit for " Mdse."

In the Journal a special column is kept for the debits (purchases) of mdse. The sum of the column is posted in total. Do not post the separate debit items of mdse.

NOTE WELL.

While this method of keeping books for a retail business is here illustrated we cannot fail to state that another and very different combination or set of books might be made to do equally well. Choosing books is exercising judgment, and we think you will display good judgment by being slow to introduce new books or new forms into a fairly well regulated office unless or until there seems to be a well defined need of a change of some kind.

CASH.—RECEIPTS.

1889.	L F	Credit Ledger Titles.	Explanation.	Mdse.		Items.		Total.	
Oct.	4		STOCK........Investment in Cash.....					1400	00
"	8	✓	MDSE ....Sales 26.32, a/c's 3.75...	30	07				
"	9		BILLS REC.....J. Jones................			25	00	25	00
"	"	✓	MDSE ....Sales....................	59	60				
	2		Total to Credit of Mdse..					89	67

1514.67

Oct. 10 BALANCE............................ 734.00

SAMPLE ACCOUNT AS IT APPEARS IN PERSONAL LEDGER.
MRS. JOHN JONES.

1889		Description of Purchases.	Debits.		Credits	
Oct.	6	To 14 lbs. G. Sugar, 1.00; 17 lbs. B.Sugar, 1.00	2			
"	"	" 1 pk. Potatoes, .25; 1 gal. Apples, .15	40			
"	8	By Cash.			1	75
"	"	To 4 lbs. Crackers, .10, .40; Sack Salt, .20 ..	60			
"	"	" 2 " Raisins, .8, .16; 5 lbs. Sugar, .10½, .53	69			
"	9	Balance of acc. per statement of acc. rend., 1.94				
"	11	By Cash.................................			1	
"	12	" Balance....			94	
			3	69	3	69

CASH.—Disbursements. Cr.

1889.	L F	Debit Ledger Titles.	Explanation.	Expense.		Items.		Total.	
Oct.	5		Fixtures .Safe 125, Store & office 130...			255			
"	"	✓	Expense ..Horse and waggon...........	200					
"	"		Private a/c.Self.......			5			
"	6		Mdse .....S. Howell & Co. gave check dis. off 3% $135.76 ; also vegetables &c. per check, 43.75...			175	44		
"	8		Mdse .....Vegetables 63.42 ; Biscuit for Hall 23.71			87	13		
"	"	✓	Expense ..Feed for horse	17	25				
"	9		Fixtures .Improving counters and bins...			23	35		
"	"		Private a/c.Self.			8			
"	"	✓	Expense,..Clerk 7.00, Messenger 2.50...	9	50				
			Total to Debit of Expense..	226	75	226	75		
								780	67
"	"		Balance..,..........................					734	00
								1514	67

Sample Page of Order Book.
Saturday, October 6th, 1889

P.L.	Mrs. John Jones, Aylmer St. 14 lbs. G. Sugar..... .... 27 " B " .... 1 pk. Potatoes ... . 1 gal. Apples................................		1 1 25 15	
			2	40
PAID.	Mrs. S. Evans, Frank St. 20 lbs. Currants, 8......................... 10 " Cheese, 9......... .... 4 oz Nutmeg, 2.........................		1 60 90 08	
			2	58
P.L.	Mrs. A. L. Davis, Brock St. 2 W. Pails, 20......................... 2 lbs. Japan Tea, 75...... .... ½ " Black " 60.................. 1 box L. Raisins, 20 lbs, 25 .... 2 lbs. Jv. Coffee, 35.............;............		40 1 50 30 5 70	
			7	90

Note.—It is not necessary to foot up this book.

SAMPLE PAGE OF JOURNAL.

OTTAWA, 4th October, 1889.

L F		Mdse. Dr.	Dr.	Cr.
	Student begins Retail Grocery busines, investing as follows:—			
✓	Mdse. Dr.......per statement.......$1,200	1200		
✓	Cash " .... " C. B............ 1,400		1400	
L F	B. Rec. " . ...J. Jones' note per B. B., due 9th inst $25		25	
L F	To Stock.............................			2625
	—————— 5— — —————			
✓	Mdse. Dr.......Bot of Jno. Macdonald on ac. acc. (Toronto) per invoice No. 1.... ....$350	350		
L F	To Jno. Macdonald..........			350
	————— " —————			
✓	Mdse. Dr........Bot. of J. S. Shorey & Co. on acc. (Montreal) per invoice No. 2 ....$500	500		
L F	To J. S. Shorey & Co....................			500
	————— " —————			
✓	Mdse. Dr........Bot. of W. J.Graham(Ottawa) for note at 2 mos per invoice No. 3...... ......$875	875		
L F	To B. Pay...........			875
	————— " —————			
✓	Mdse. Dr........Bot. of W. T. Walker & Son (Toronto) for note at 2 mos per invoice No. 4....$175	175		
L F	To B. Pay............................			175
	—.———— " ————			
✓	Private acc. Dr... Provisions $3.75		3 75	
L F	To Mdse.......			3 75
	(Red ink) Amounts carried forward..	3100	1428 75	4528 75

SET 1—RETAIL.

Books used :—Journal, Bill Book, Ledger, Order Book, Personal Ledger, Special Cash Book.

4th, 1889.

Student begins Retail Grocery business, investing as follows :—Mdse., per statement, $1200 ; cash per C B., $1400 ; bills rec., J. Jones' note, due Jan. 9th, $25., per Bill Book. [J.-C. B.]

5.

Bot. of Jno. Macdonald, (Toronto, Ont,) on ac. Mdse., per Invoice, $350. [J.]

Bot. of J. S. Shorey & Co., Montreal, Que., on ac. Mdse, per Invoice, $500. [J.]

Bot. of W. J. Graham, Ottawa, for note @ 4 months, Mdse. per Invoice, $875. [J.-B. B.]

Bot. of W. T. Walker & Son, Toronto, for note @ 2 months. Mdse, per Invoice, $175. [J.-B. B.]

Have paid bills for the following :—Safe, $125 ; horse and wagon, $200 ; store and office fixtures, $130. [C. B.]

For own use, cash, $5.00 ; Provisions $3.75. (C. B.-J.)

Deposited balance of cash on hand in the Merchants Bank. (Memo on Stub of Check Book only.)

6.

The following charges are found in the Order Book unpaid :—Mrs. John Jones, Aylmer Street, 14 ℔s. G. Sugar, $1.00 ; 17 ℔s. B. Sugar, $1.00 ; 1 peck Potatoes, 25c. ; 1 gal. Apples, 15c. (P. L.)

Mrs. A. L. Davis, Brock Street, 2 W. Pails @ 20c ; 2 ℔s Japan Tea, @ 75c. ; ½ ℔ Black Tea, @ 60c. ; 1 box L. Raisins, 20 ℔s @ 25c.; 2 ℔s Java Coffee, @ 35c. (P. L.)

Mrs. E. B. Stone, Brock Street, 14 ℔s. G. Sugar, $1.00 ; 2 ℔s. Loaf Sugar @ 20c. ; 1 bag Potatoes 75c. ; 14 ℔s Haddie @ 11c. (P.L.)

Mrs. R. E. Wood, Water Street, 10 ℔s P. Butter, @ 23c. ; ¼ ℔ A. Spice, @ 40c. ; (1) 10 ℔. sack F. Salt, 20c., 3 doz. Eggs @ 14c. ; 1 Lem. Ext., 25c., 1 Can Oysters, 40c. ; 2 ℔s. Crackers @ 10c. (P. L.)

7.

Memo :—Paid, per check, Invoice of Provisions bought of S. Howell & Co., Ottawa, @ 30 days, amounting to $135.76 ; Dis. off 3°/₀. [C. B.]

NOTE.—This discount being allowed off the bill and the bill being paid before any entry has been made of the transaction, we therefore take no further notice of the discount. Enter the net amount $131.69 only.

Slips on File as follows:—Vegetables, Poultry, &c., bought at Market, paid, per check, $43.75. (C. B)

Order Book Charges :—Mrs. J. R. Stratton, Aylmer Street, 3 lbs. Mackeral @ 8c.; 11½ lbs. chicken @ 12c. ; 13 lbs G.Sugar, $1.00; 2½ lbs. L. Sugar @ 20c. ; 5 lbs. Honey Soap, @ 17c. ; 1 gal. Coal Oil 30c.

8

Memo:—Bot. at Market; Vegetables, Butter, Poultry &c., for which I paid, per check, am't, $63.42. Invoice of Biscuit from J.Hall, town, $23.71, paid per check. Feed for ho se, $17.25, per check. (C.B.)

Slips on File:—Rec'd on a/c., Mrs. Jones, Cash $1.75 ; Mrs. Stone, $2.00. Cash Sales, per C. D., $26.32 ; add this to the amount received on accounts, $3.75, making the credit to Mdse. $30.07

NOTE :—Credit each account in the Personal Ledger, and you add the sums paid you to the cash sales for the day, and thus in the Cash Book, credit Mdse, by the total amount. The reason you credit Mdse. now, is because you did not credit Mdse. when the goods were sold.

The following charges in the Order Book are still unpaid : Mrs. E. L. Wood, 10 lbs. G.Sugar @ 12½ c.; 1 lb. Japan Tea @ 45c. ; 2 lbs. Biscuit @ 12c.; 4 lbs. F. Haddie @ 12½c.; ½ Gal. Coal Oil @ 35c.

Mrs. John Jones, 4 lbs. Crackers @ 10c.; 1 Sack Salt, 20c. ; 2 lbs. Raisins @ 08c.; 5 lbs. Sugar @ 10½c.

Mrs. A. L. Davis, 1 lb. Pepper, 25c.; 1 lb. Starch, 10c.; ¼ lb Soda @ 10c.; ½ lb. Crm. Tartar @ 20c.; 2 oz. Allspice, 05c.; 2 lbs C.Fish @ 7c.; 1 Can Friend's B. Powder, 25c.

Mrs. J. D. Macdonald, Rubidge Street, 1 Can Salmon, 18c.; 1 oz Cloves, 05c.; 5 lbs Butter @ 22c.; 25 lbs. Pastry Flour @ 3c.; ½ Gal. Coal Oil @ 35c.; 1 doz Eggs, @ 12c.

9

Rec'd payment for J. Jones' note.

Paid, per check, for carpenter work on counters and bins, $23.35.

NOTE :—This item should be charged to "Fixtures" because it makes bins, &c., more valuable and is of the nature of a permanent improvement. If, however, the work on bins, &c., were of the nature of repairs, then Expense a/c. would have been charged.

Slips on File:—For private use, cash, $8.00; goods, $7.50

Paid Clerk one week's wages, $7.00, and messenger, $2.50

NOTE:—If there were many hands employed it would be well to open a "Wages" or "Salary" a/c. But here in this case you debit "Expense."

Cash Sales:—Per C. D., $59.60

The following charges in the Order Book are still unpaid : Mrs. J. English, Water Street, 1 box Starch, 6 lbs., 45c.; 1 bbl Apples, $2.00 1 pk E. R. Potatoes, 25c., 1 Lem Extract 12c. 2 doz. Eggs @ 12c.

Mrs. J. I. Davidson, Rubidge Street, 5 lbs. L. Raisins @ 23c ; 1 nest (3) W. Tubs, 75c., $1.00, $1.50; 2 lbs. Japan Tea @ 60.; 1 lb Black Tea, 45c.

Mrs. R. E. Wood, 1 box soap, $2.10 ; 1 bbl. Apples, $3.60; 1 bbl. XXX Flour, $6.75.

Deposited cash, $90.00

NOTE:—Render statements of a/c. to Mrs. Jones and Mrs. Stone. Balance O.B. and carry balance down to debit side.

11.

Paid cash for painting counters, $6.25.

Bot. Fruit, Vegetables, &c., per check, $13.75.

Rec'd on a/c., Mrs. Jones $1.00; Mrs. Davis, $5.00 ; Mrs. R. E, Wood, $6.00; Mrs. Stratton $3.00.

The following charges in the Order Book are still unpaid :— Mrs. Stratton, 25 lbs. O. Meal, 70c.; 1 qt. Oysters, 40c ; 2 lbs. Biscuit @ 10c.; 1 bbl. Apples, $3.25 ; 2 crates Peaches @ $3.25.

Mrs. Geo. A. Cox, 1 bbl Flour, XXX, $6.75'; 1 bbl. Apples, $3 25; 1 box L. Raisins, $5.15 ; 2 lbs. J. Tea, 60c.; 1 lb Black Tea, 45c.; 6 lbs. Mackeral @ 8c.

Mrs. E. B. Stone, 3 lbs. V. Grapes @ 15c.; 1 lb Honey, 20c.; 1 gal. C. Oil, 35c.; 1 pk. Potatoes, 25c.; 1 lb Java Coffee. 45c.; 2 lbs. crackers @ 12½c.; 2 lbs. Chicken @ 12½c.

Paid cash for horse-shoeing, $2.00 ; postage 25c.

Paid cash for bill heads and envelopes, $2.50.

Cash Sales:—Per C. D., $136.71. Rec'd on ac. as above, $15.00. Total cash received, $151.71.

12.

Memo:—Paid for coal, $7.00, per check. Paid for stove and fixtures, $37.35, per check. Paid by check for ma 'ing coal bin, $2.00,

NOTE:—Charge "Fixtures" account for all except coal which is an expense item.

Order Book Charges :—Mrs. Wm. Leck, Hunter Street, 10 lbs. G. Sugar, $1.00 ; 25 lbs O. Meal, 70c.; 1 ℔ J. Tea, 60c.; 1 ℔ Java Coffee, 45c.; 5 lbs L. Raisins @ 23c.

Mrs. W. H. Thompson, Reid Street, 1 gal. Syrup, 85c.; 2 W. Pails @ 20c.; 1 Market Basket, 10c., 1 Lem. Ext., 15c.

NOTE :—Render statements of acs. to Mrs. Cox and Mrs. R. E. Wood.

The following sums were rec'd on account :—Mrs. Cox, $10.00 ; Mrs. R. E. Wood, $6.00 ; Mrs. Stratton, $5.00 ; Mrs. Stone , $2.00.

Cash sales, $295.50 ; total cash received to-day, $295.50 + $23.00 = $318.50.

Deposited $450.00. Remitted checks to John Macdonald and J. S. Shorey & Co. in full of account.

NOTE :—Post entries, take a Trial Balance and close fluctuating accounts into "Loss and Gain." Place Inventories on credit side of accounts to which they belong, in red ink, and after closing these accounts bring down Inventories to debit side of account, using black ink. Next close the net gain or net loss into stock, this shows the net worth at the time of admitting your partners (which will be done in the Wholesale Grocery set). Next close Stock and bring down balance in black ink to credit side. The sum of the debit and credit Ledger balances should be equal. Put personal a/c Inventory on credit side of Mdse. along with amount of unsold goods. Private accounts close into Stock.

Inventories :
 Mdse $2820.75   Net Loss $ 27.41
 Personal ac's 44.48   Net Worth 2573.34
 Expense 200.00   Footing of T.B. 5947.90
 Fixtures 275.00

Accounts to be opened in the Ledger with number of lines required for each.

Stock, 5 ; Bills Rec., 2 ; Bills Pay, 4 ; Mdse., 7 ; J.Macdonald, 2 ; J. S.Shorey & Co., 3 ; Expense, 4 ; Private ac. 4 ; Fixtures 7 ; Loss and Gain, 4.

QUESTIONS.

COVERING RETAIL EXAMINATION.

What books are used? Give the advantages of using special columns. Describe the use of the P. L. Distinguish between expense and private a/cs. Why is no cash a/c kept in this set?

SPECIAL COLUMN JOURNAL.

OTTAWA, Ont., Jan'y 4th, 1890.

Mdse. Dr.	Cash Dr.	Exp'ns Dr.	S'ndr's Dr.	l f		l f	S'ndr's Cr	Cash Cr.	Mdse. Cr.
400					2 Mdse. Dr.				
	100				2 Cash Dr				
			200		3 B. Rec. Dr......				
					To Mdse......	2			700
					Sold to J. Jones, red'd in paym't				
					---3---				
26					2 Mdse. Dr.......				
			1		5 Expense Dr.....				
					To Cash......	2		27	
					Bot of S. Evans, per invoice No. 1; freight $1.				
					---5---				
		1 50			5 Expense Dr.....				
					To Cash......	2		1 50	
					Office books.				
					---8---				
	20 10				2 Cash Dr........				
					To Mdse......	2			20 10
					Sales.				
					---9---				
	200				2 Cash Dr........				
					To B. Rec....	3	200		
		2 50	2 50		J. Smith's note.				
	320 10		320 10				28 50	28 50	
426			426				720 10		720
			948 60				948 60		

NOTE.—This set may be worked with a Journal of this kind if thought advisable. An ordinary retail business is presumed; othewise we advise the books indicated at beginning of set. If this book be used, the ordinary Journal and Cash Book may be dispensed with.

1889.			CONSIGNMENT "A".			Cr.
Sept.	9	✓	Cash, 100 bu. wheat @ 75¢...............	75		
"	29	✓	Cash, 100 bu. wheat @ 50¢...............	50		125
						125

REMARKS
— ON —
SHIPMENT AND CONSIGNMENT SET 2.
BUSINESS, ADVERSE.—Single Proprietorship.

The Journal, Commission Sales Ledger and C. B. are kept in this Set as principal books from which the posting is done direct.

The Commission Invoice Book is used to enter abstracts of invoices received. Enter the Consignments as 1, 2, 3 &c. Invoices should be checked over with goods, and boxes, packages, parcels, &c., marked with distinguished numbers. Different consignments from same person should be marked A, B, &c. No posting from this book.

Any entries pertaining to consignments must be made in the C.S.L.

Entries involving cash, are entered in the C. B. All others in the Journal.

When entries are partially cash, the entry is made complete in the Journal and then the cash entered in the C.B.

Special columns may at any time be added to any of these books in actual practice, when the posting is heavy and it is deemed advisable to add special columns.

When a consignment is received, check over the items with the Invoice received, and mark the goods in such a way that it will afterwards be easily seen where they belong. The Invoice should be folded, filed and pasted into what may be called a Commission Invoice Book. In the Commission Sales Book, or Comission Sales Ledger, open the ac. and simply state that the Consignment has been received, giving date. No Journal entry, that is, no debit or credit is affected yet, unless you either pay or assume charges, freight or the like, at time of receiving goods.

105

SAMPLE PAGES OF THE COMMISSION SALES LEDGER.

1889.   Dr.   No. 1, TAYLOR & CO'S.   (Stittsville.)

Sept.	7	✓	Cash, freight (on 200 bu. wheat recd @ 50¢..	20	
"	29		Commission, 3% on sales $125.	3	75
"	"		Insurance, 1% on sales $125.	1	25
"	"		Storage, 1 cent per bushel on 100 bushels...	1	00	26
"	29	✓	Cash, proceeds remitted................			99
						125

NOTE.—Cash is not posted from C. S. L. as it is placed in the C. B., and there the entry is also checked (✓) off. Cash acct. not being opened in this Ledger.

SET II.—COMMISSION.

Sept. 1st.   Student has leased store on Sparks St. and commenced business as Commission Merchant and Shipper and agrees to pay a rent of $600.00 per annum.

   NOTE:—My Capital on beginning business is $2000, Cash. Goods on hand $10,000, for which I owe McKay & Co. $10,000.

"   I insure my stock for $10,000 @ ¼ %, paying premium in cash. (C. B.)

"   Deposited Cash in College Bank $2,000.00. (C. B.)

"   Bot. of McKay & Co. on acct. :
     Flour and Feed as per Inv. $678.00. (J.)

Sept. 4th   Sold Wm. Switzer on 90 days acct. :
     10 bbls. Flour @ $5.00,
     300 lbs. Oatmeal @ 2c. (J.)

"   Bot of Martin & Co. on note @ 2 mos. :
     500 bbls. Flour @ $3.80. (J.—B. B)

"   Sold Jas. Smith on note at 1 mo. :
     50 bbls. Flour @ $5.00. (J.—B. B.)

Sept. 7th.   Had Smith's note discounted and
     proceeds received by check on Bank of Toronto, $245.00. (C. B.—B. B.)

"   Bot. of Jackson & Co. on note @ 1 mo. :
     700 bu. Barley @ 60c. (J.—B. B.)

Sept. 7th.	Ordered of McKay & Co. Mdse. as per Inv. amounting to $80.00 and gave in payment check on College Bank. (J.—C. B.)
"	Shipped to Willoughby & Co. Chicago: 200 bbls. Flour valued @ 3.80. (J.)
"	Rec'd. of Taylor & Co., Stittsville, for sale on their ac. and risk: 200 bush. Wheat valued at 50c. bush., and paid freight in Cash $20.00. C. S. L. and C. B.
Sept. 8th.	Sold for Cash to-day, per order book $250.23. (C. B.)
"	Paid for circulars and postage, in cash $12.15. (C. B.)
Sept. 9th.	Shipped to McKay & Co. to be sold on my acct. and risk 100 bbls. Flour valued @ $3.80. (J.)
"	Sold G. P. Brown shipment to McKay before receiving ac. sales, gave Bill of Sale, and notified McKay & Co. to forward shipment to Brown. (J.)
"	Sold from Taylor & Co's consignment, for cash. 100 bush. Wheat @ 75c. (C. B.)
"	Shipped to Brown & Co. Montreal 500 bush Barley valued @ 60c. (J.)
Sept. 10th.	Drew on Wm. Switzer @ 20 days through College Bank, to balance a/c.

TAKE OFF TRIAL BALANCE, AFTER POSTING.

Sept. 11th.	Admitted J. N. Taylor and J. Law as partners with Capital of $1,000 each, Gains and Losses to be shared according to investment.
"	Hired Thomas Good, and Geo. Abbot as clerks at $8 per week, and Frank Stowe as bookkeeper at $50.00 per month.
"	Sold Wm. Gee for Cash: 100 bu. Barley at 75c.
12	Bot. of Martin & Co. on 3 mos. time: 500 bu wheat @ 60c.
"	Sold James Smith, on account. 150 bbls Flour @ $4.50
13	Had my note for $130 discounted at Bank and for ½ proceeds rec'd a certificate of deposit bearing 5% int., the remainder to be placed at my credit.

Sept. 13th. Sold James Stitt for note @ 3 mos.
Flour and Feed as per invt'y $378.00
" Sold W. M. Little on 3 mos. credit
500 bu Barley @ 80c.
14 Bot. of McKay & Co. on 2 mos. credit :
75 bbls. Flour @ $4.00
" Exchange with W. Smith my note @ 5 days for $100 for his for same time and amount.
15 Took out a policy of Insurance on Store, Fixtures and stock for $3,000.00 at 80c. per 100
16 Purchased a 60 day bill of Exchange on London for £3 8s 6d. @ $4.82.

NOTE:—The value of a £ Sterling is $4.86⅔, but as this bill is paid for 63 days before it matures, Bankers allow interest to the purchaser, who thus makes in interest more than the cost of Exchange. Hence the quotation at less than actual value of sterling money.

18 Paid for advertising in 2 City papers, $28.00.
" J. N. Taylor and J. Law each withdrawn one-third of their Investment in Cash.
" Bot. of Martin & Co. on note @ 4 mos.
300 bbls. Flour at $3.75
" Bot. of McKay & Co.:
100 bu. Rye @ 40c.
100 bu. Barley @ 60c., and gave in payment Smith's accommodation note.
" Had bill of Exchange collected through Bank of Toronto @ ¼% Exchange. Proceeds in Cash.
" Shipped Martin & Co. to be sold on our acct and risk :
100 bush Rye valued at 40c.
19 Rec'd from MacIntosh & Co., Montreal to be sold on their acct and risk : 300 bbls. Flour valued at $4 25
" Paid MacKay & Co's. Bill of 1st, inst. by draft on College Bank which I purchased by check.
" Sold MacIntosh & Co's. consgt of 300 bbls. Flour at $5 per bbl. and rendered acct. Sales' Commission 2%, storage 4c. per bbl.

NOTE:—In this entry there are two journal entries involved. When the sale is made the cash should be debited and the consgt. credited. When the acct. sales is rendered the consgt. is debited and then closed by crediting Commission, Storage and MacIntosh, by the net proceeds. You credit MacIntosh with the net proceeds because you retain them in your possession, subject to his order.

Sept. 19th. Shipped Craig & Co. Toronto, to be sold on our acct. and risk : 100 bush. Barley, valued at 60c.

" Drew on James Smith, through Bank of Toronto for amount of his bill of 12th inst.

" Bot. of McKay & Co. for check :
400 bush. Oats @ 55c.
200 bbls. Flour @ $3.50.

20 Had Jas. Stitts' note discounted at Bank 30 days before due and proceeds placed to our credit.

" Rec'd acct sales from Craig & Co. Toronto of 75 bush barley @ 86⅔c. Pro. in cash $65.00.

" Rec'd from Blythe & Co. to be sold on their account and risk 75 bbls. Flour valued @ 3.50.

" Sold from Blyth & Co's Const. :
50 bbls. Flour at $4 and rec'd. in payment a certified check.

" Paid clerks and book-keeper in full ; keeping the acct of each separately.

" TAKE OFF A TRIAL BALANCE AFTER HAVING POSTED UP TO DATE.

Sept. 21st. Deposited in College Bank $100.

" Rec'd from Taylor & Co. Stittsville to be sold on their acct. and risk :
1000 bush. Wheat valued at 55c.
Pd. freight in Cash $12.

" Took to my own acct. by consent of Taylor & Co. the goods belonging to his to-day's consignment.

" Rec'd. from MacIntosh & Co. Montreal to be sold on their acct. and risk : 500 bbls. Flour valued at $3.85 and paid freight in Cash $38.00.

" Bot. of McKay & Co. for check :
300 bbls. Flour at $3.00.

22 Shipped to Jenkins & Co. Montreal the Consignment rec'd. from McIntosh & Co. and had goods Insured at ⅓ °/. of value. Paid premium in cash.

" Shipped Charleston & Co. Quebec to be sold on our acct. and risk : 200 bbls. Flour valued at $3.00

Sept. 22nd. Shipped Burke & Co., Brockville, to be sold on our acct. and risk : 1000 bush. Wheat valued at 55c.
23 Rec'd of Brown & Co., Buckingham, to be sold on their acct and risk :
560 bush Indian Corn valued at 30c.
" J. N. Taylor withdraws from the firm ¼ of his original investment in Cash.
" Rec'd of Taylor & Co.,Stittsville, to be sold on his acct. and risk : 280 bags Gr. Flour valued at $1.20.
24 Bot. of Martin & Co on 4 months time :
350 bbls Flour @ $3.75.
" Rec'd from Burke & Co., Brockville, an Account Sales of our shipment to them. Our net proceeds received in Cash. $567.00.
" Shipped to McKay & Co. to be sold on our acct. and risk 200 bbls. Flour valued at $3.75
" Sold Jackson & Co. for check
150 bbls. Flour at $4.50.
25 Sold James Smith on 60 days time, 150 bags Gr. Flour at $1.60 from Taylor & Co's Consignment.
" Had our note for $400.00 discounted at Bank and proceeds placed to our credit. Rate 7%. Time, 3 mos.
26 Sold Switzer & Co. for an endorsed note at 3 mos. from Taylor & Co's. Consignment :
130 bags Gr. Flour @ $1.75.
" Had Switzer & Co's note discounted and proceeds placed to our credit $223.00.
28 Rec'd from Blythe & Co to be sold on their acct. and risk 200 bbls. Flour valued at $3.50
" Shipped to Burke & Co., Brockville, to be sold on our acct. and risk the consignment rec'd from Blythe & Co.
29 Sold for check all Mdse on Hand for $600.
" 1 Take off a continued trial balance.
" 2 Take off a statement of Losses and Gains.
" 3 Take off a statement of Accts. Receivable.

Accounts to be opened in the Ledger with the number of lines required for each. Leave 6 lines each for the following accounts : Stock, Mdse., B. Receivable, B. Payable ; 3 lines each for the others except Loss and Gain which should be allowed 12 lines each.

CONTINUED TRIAL BALANCE.

No.	LEDGER TITLES.	F.	Sept. 10, 188 DR.	Sept. 10, 188 CR.	188 Sept. 20.	Sept. 30, 188 DR.	Sept. 30, 188 CR.
1	Stock............	1	10000	12000		10000	12000
2	Cash.............	1	2570 23	2057 15		6426 70	3108 32
3	Bills Receivable.....	2	306	250		1475 51	874 51
4	Bills Payable	2		2320			3545
5	Mdse.............	3	13078	1996 23		15823	3624 23
6	Balance from C.S.L..			55			255
7	College Bank.......	5	2000	80		2437 21	1678
8	McKay & Co	5		10678		678	10978
9	William Switzer.... ✓	6					
10	G. P. Brown	6	380			380	
11	Shipt. to Willoughby..	7	760			760	
12	Shipt. to Brown & Co.	7	300			300	
13	Shipt. to McKay... ✓	7					
14	Discount	8	5			14 69	
15	Expense	8	37 15			127 19	
			29436 38	29436 38			
16	J. N. Taylor........				9	583 33	1000
17	J. Law.............				9	333 33	1000
18	Martin & Co........				9		300
19	Jas Smith..........				10		
20	Certificate of Deposit..				10	61 10	
21	W. M. Little.......				10	400	
22	Commission				11		30
23	Storage				11		12
24	Shipt. to Craig				11	60	65
25	McIntosh.				12		1458
26	Shipt. to Martin				14	40	
27	Advertising.........				14	28	
						39928 06	39928 06

NOTE.— The student is expected to find all these results independently; and to find the results of the posting on the 20th Sept. as well.

QUESTIONS,

ON CONSIGNMENTS AND SHIPMENTS.

What is a consgt. ? What entry is made upon receiving a consgt. ? How is it closed? When is a shipt. debited? Why do consgts. close when disposed of? What does the difference in the sides of a shipt. show? Do you post consgts. to the General Ledger? If not, how is the trial balance made to balance?

REMARKS
— ON —
CASH JOURNAL, SET 3.
A CONVENIENT METHOD FOR SOCIETY BOOK-KEEPING, AND WHEN BUSINESS IS NEARLY ALL CASH.

To save time and labor when the receipts are mainly cash :

1. Find your Journal entry of each transaction.

2. If cash be the only debit, enter all the credit items on the debit side of the C. B.

3. If cash be the only credit, enter all the debit items on the credit side of the C. B.

4. It no cash is involved in the entry, put the credits on the debit and the debits on the credit side. In this way you increase both sides equally and thus leave cash account undisturbed.

5. If one of the debits or credits be cash, strike it out and enter all the remaining debits on the credit side of the C. B.

6. In Posting to the Ledger transfer the balance of cash only to Cash a/c.

NOTE:—The Student should work out this set by taking all the entries from and beginning with No. 39 on page 58. The Cash Journal should be balanced five times, as follows: after 59th, 65th, 54th, 60th and 65th entries.

The following accounts should be opened : Student, 4 lines ; W. Green, 4 ; Brouse Bros, 2 ; Cash, 2 ; Musgrove. 2 ; Mdse., 6 ; Bills Rec., 4 ; Bills Pay., 4 ; E. Robinson, 2 ; Sinclair, Jack & Co., 3 ; J. Hope & Co. 2 ; J Gibson, 2; Interest, 2 ; J. Lang, 2 ; Expense, 2 ; Exchange, 2 ; J. Macdonald, 2 ; Discount, 2 ; H. W. Kirby, 2 ; J. G. Blaine, 2 ; Fixtures, 2 ;

QUESTIONS,
ON CASH METHOD.

To what kind of business is the Cash Journal adapted ? What are its advantages ? What does the sum of each side represent ? What does the balance show ? How are time sales entered ? How are part payment entries made ?

REMARKS
— ON —
MANUFACTURING SET 4.
PARTNERSHIP BUSINESS, PROSPROUS.

Books Required.—Journal, C. B., Sales Book, Ledger, as principal books; and a Hands Register, B. E , Collateral Security Register and Collateral Receipt Book as auxiliaries.

Journ.:—Contains all entries that cannot properly be made in other books.

Cash Book :—This book is kept as usual, excepting that the debit column on the left hand page is used for entering all cash sales of merchandise. All "Regular" bills have four months to run, and if settled for within 30 days, the debtor is allowed a discount of 5 per cent.

Be sure in such cases to credit the purchaser in the C. B. for the whole amount of the account, and debit Discount account on the other side of the book, for the discount. When the C. B. is balanced carry the footing of the Mdse. column to the credit side of Mdse. ac. in the Ledger.

Goods sold for "Net Cash" are supposed to be settled in 30 days and are, after that time, if unpaid, subject to draft at sight. "Regular" bills are subject to draft after 4 months, or at 4 months from date of sale.

Prove the C. B. every evening, it need not be closed oftener than once a week.

Bill Book:—Needs teacher's special attention. Ask.

Sales Book :—This book contains all sales. The debits are made direct; the Mdse. is credited at the end of each week. (In practice at the end of each month is usually the time for posting.)

Hands Register:—This is a book ruled like a continued trial balance. The Cr. column contains the daily, weekly, monthly, or yearly wage, earned by each employee, and the Dr. column contains the amount of value actually received by each one. The difference in the columns must show how the accounts stand.

A Stock account is opened in this set instead of partner's accounts. This saves space, time, and keeps the curious from being unduly enlightened.

A Plant Account is one kept to ascertain the cost, wear and tear, etc., of the machinery and tools required in a manufactory. This a/c should be charged at the close of the year with intere t on the money invested and the wear on machinery, etc.

The Collateral Security Register is a book into which full particulars are entered respecting long time paper received for machinery or manufactured wares sold. In the case of Agricultural manufactories, the goods are usually sold on long time paper, which are often attached to the 4 months paper of the Manufacturer and held by the Bank as Collateral security. In this case it is not the farmer's note that is discounted, it is the manufacturers'.

The Collateral Receipt Book is a book in which is a description of all the long time paper in the hands of the bank and contains also the receipts signed by the Bank showing the paper in his possesion.

The Counter Books :—In many Manufactories there is a book lying on the counter in which all transactions are entered by the salesmen, or clerk, and from which the Journal, Sales Book and C. B. are written up. A convenient plan is to have three different Counter Books, one for sales, another for purchases and another for miscelleanous items.

NOTE:—We herewith give forms of Collateral Register and Collateral Receipt Book. The use of each will be readily seen from these forms.

OTTAWA, August 23rd, 1889.

Col. Reg. Folio.	RECEIVED of Campbell & Co'y, this 23rd day of August, 1889, the following promissory notes for credit of his Collateral Account at this Ontario Bank :	
	Watson & Co , Ottawa, due 2/9/89	400
	G. G Gold & Son, Almonte, " 30/8/89	200
	Signed, C. MAGILL, Mgr. O. B.	

J. CAMPBELL & Co.—WEEKLY TIME BOOK
For the Week ending Saturday, December 6th, 1890.

No.	NAMES.	M	T	W	T	F	S	Total.	Rate. Per Day	Extra.	Amount.	Remarks.
(a)	THE SHOP HANDS.											
1	Dunlap	P	P	P!	P	P	P	6	$3 50		$21 00	Steady, but rather slow.
2	Young	P!	P	P	P	P	P	6	3 50	2 50	23 50	
3	Gillespie	P	P	A	A	P	½	4½	4 00	7 60	25 60	
4	Hamilton	P	P	A	A	A	P	3	4 00	1 00	13 00	Unsteady.
5	Morton	P	A	P	P!	P	P	6	5 00	3 80	33 80	
6	Case	P	P	A	A	A	½	1½	4 00	4 00	10 00	Should be dismissed. He is intemperate and idle.
7	Toby	P	P	?	P	P!	A	4	4 00	0 60	16 60	
8	Rogers	P	P	A	P	P	P	5	5 00	4 00	29 00	
9	Long	P!	½	P!	P	P	P	5½	5 00	1 50	29 00	
10	Stenson	P	P	A	½	P	P	4½	3 00	11 00	24 50	Fast workman, but irregular.
11	Jackson (Foreman)	P	P	P	P	P!	P	6	8 00	2 00	50 00	
(b)	WAREHOUSE HANDS.											
1	Currie	P	P	P	P	P	P	6			60 00	Book-keeper.
2	Moxon	P!	P	P!	½	P	P	6			16 00	Assistant.
3	Davis	P	P	P	P!	P!	P	6			36 00	Salesman.
4	May	P!	P	P	P!	P	P	6			40 00	

NOTE:—"!" after "P" in the Time Book means "late."

SALES BOOK.

OTTAWA, Ont., 1st December, 1890.

Dec.	L	F		Regular.		Net.		Total	
Dec.	1	12	Cooper & Haight., Dr., (Picton.)						
			2 No. 33 Walnut Beds.	21					
			2 " " Wood Top Press..	34					
			2 " 2 Towel Racks	3	30				
			4 " 80 Chairs...................			1	84		
			24 " 49½ "			30			
			24 " 57 "			18		108	14
"	1	13	Geo. Lapum, Dr., (Fairport.)						
			6 Best Sideboard Beds............			12	60		
			6 High H. D. Cots			15	30		
			6 Low do.			14	40		
			2 Improved Con. Chairs...........			5	70		
			48 No. 72 Light do.			22			
			24 " Dark do.			11			
			8 " 61 " do.			3	84	84	84
"	1	14	H. Brennan, Dr., (Ottawa.)						
			12 No. 36 Maple Chairs............			21	60	21	60
"	2	15	D. Pierson, Dr., (Toronto.)						
			12 No. 25 Chairs.			14	4		
			27 " 72 "			10	50		
			12 " 57 "			9		33	90
"	2	16	Lee Bros., Dr., (Oxford.)						
			2 No 33 Walnut W. T. Suit	69	50				
			Tete in Jute.......................	44					
			Ford Rockers.....................	22					
			Arm Chair.			10		145	50
				193	80	200	18	393	98

NOTE.—Continue entries in sales book as illustrated above. Add at the foot of each page, and carry footings forward as in journal.

NOTES HELD AS COLLATERAL SECURITY ON COLLATERAL SECUR

When Rec'd	No.	PROMISSOR.	OCCUPATION.	ADDRESS.	Due Date.
1889 Aug.	23	Weston & Co......	....	Ottawa............	2/9/89
"	"	Leask & Co.......	....	Toronto...........	30/8/89
"	24	W. Griffin........	....	Otterville..... ...	10/9/89
"	"	H. Johnstone	....	Drumbo....	9/9/89

PIECE WORK TIME BOOK—PIECES, WAGES, PAY.

No.	Name.	DATE—DECEMBER 6TH, 1890.				DATE.			
		Quantity	Rate.	Amount.	Rec. Pay	Quantity.	Rate	Amount.	R'd Pay. Initials.
1	Case.	Chairs 40	10	$4 00.	J. C.				

PAY ROLL FOR THE MONTH ENDING JULY 27TH, 1890.

No.	Names.	Occupation	WAGES, Rate per Month.	Days.	Am't.	Deductions	Amt.	Net Am't	Signatures.
1	Jas. Jones.	Millwright.	$ c 78 00	25	$75 50	$ $ $ c. 10 3 5 50	18 50	56 50	J. Jones.

ITY REGISTER.
ACCOUNT OF A.R. COOK vs. STANDARD BANK.

Amt. of notes to be entered as a debit.	Amt. of note taken out to be entered as a credit.	Balance of notes on hand.	Notes given favor of Bank.	Bank notes retired.	Date when paid or given up	FATE OF.
400			500	500		
200	200		1000		30/8/'89	A. (This is the Book-keeper's initial for the $200 note.)
600			600			
625						

SET IV.—MANUFACTURING.

—— 1, 18 ——

Resources of J. Campbell & Co., Furniture Manufacturers :

Real Estate :—Manufactory $30,000.00 ; Warehouse $40,000.00, Total $70,000.00.

Merchandise :—Manufactured $15,000.00 ; Lumber $16,000.00 ; Hardware $2,800.00 ; Fabrics, etc., $1,400.00 ; Varnishes, Oil, etc., $1,000.00. Total $36,200.00.

Machinery and Tools :—$10,000.00; *Office Fixtures*, Safe, Desk, etc., $700. *Ontario Bank*, on deposit, $8.973.68; *Cash* in Safe $422.28.

Bills Receivable :—Note of R. Burns, Toronto, at 3 months from Sept. 1st., with interest, $1,730.00. Note of J. K. Pierce, Hamilton, at 3 mos. from Sept. 6th, with interest, $1,900.00. Note of F. Wilton, Kingston, at 2 mos. from Oct. 19th, with interest, $3,489.00. Note of B. Longly, Ottawa, at 3 mos. from Nov. 15th, with interest, $856.30. Total $7,975.30. Interest accrued on above notes, $79.58.

Personal Accounts:—C. Gardiner, Brockville, Mdse. bought on regular, Nov. 3, $2,873.70. S. Jones, Perth, Mdse. bought Nov. 5, regular, $2,307.70, net, $434.86. Cooper & Haight, Picton, Mdse. bought Nov. 19, regular, $469.00 net, $2,235.90. W. Green, Wellington, Mdse. bought Nov. 21, regular, $2,286.50 ; net, $146.22. Warner & Stone, Belleville, Mdse. bought Nov. 7, net, $432.80. H. Brennan, Ottawa, Mdse. bought Nov. 10, regular, $368.60 ; ne. $390.20. Lee Bros., Oxford, Mdse. bought Nov. 3 gular, $2,846.00. Geo. Lapum, Fairport, Mdse. bought Nov. 16, regular, $166.36 ; net, $82.24. D.

Pierson, Toronto, Mdse. bought Nov. 23, regular, $236.90; net, $122.34.
H. Fraser, Picton, Mdse. bought Nov. 25; net, $2,246.36. Total Resources, $141,396.52.

Note:—Keep the sum of the "Reg" and the sum of the "Net" items apart both in the Journal and Ledger.

Sold Cooper & Haight, Picton, 2 No. 33 Walnut Beds, $21.00 ; 2 No. 33 Wal't Wood Top Dressers, $34.00 ; 2 No. 2 Walnut Towel Racks, $3.30, regular; 4 No. 80 chairs, $1.84 ; 24 No. 49½ chairs, $30.00 ; 24 No. 57 chairs, $18.00, net.

H. Brennan, Ottawa, 12 No. 30 Maple Chairs, $21.60, net.

Geo. Lapum, Fairport, 6 Best Side-board Beds, $12.60 ; 6 High H. D. Cots, $15.30 ; 6 Low do., $14.40 ; 2 Imp. Cong. Chairs, $5.70 ; 48 No. 72 Light Chairs, $22.00 ; 24 No. 72 Dark Chairs, $11.00 ; 8 No. 61 chairs, $3.84, net.

Cash Sales:—R. Kerr, 2 C. Suites, $72.00. J. Kemp, 2 Pat. Rocker, $44.00. D. Rogers, 2 Parlor Suites, $288.00.

2,

Sold D. Pierson, Toronto, 12 No. 25 chairs, $14.40 ; 24 No. 72 chairs, sing. round, light, $10.50 ; 12 No. 57 ch., $9.00, net.

Lee Bros. Oxford, 2 No. 33 Wal't Wood Top Suit, $69.50 ; 2 Tete in Jute, $44.00; 2 Ford Rocker, $22.00, regular; 2 Arm Chair, $10., net.

H. Fraser, Picton, 4 No. 4 Soft Wood Beds, $13.00; 4 No. 25½ ch, $16.00 ; 4 No. 24 Ash and Walnut Beds, $18.00 ; 36 No. 57 chairs in white (unfinished) $54.00 ; 6 No. 33 Ash and Walnut Beds, $36.00 ; 8 No. 309 ch., $8.00, net.

Received check from C. Gardiner, Brockville, for the amount of his bill of Nov. 3, $2,873.70, less the regular discount, 5 per cent.

Bought, for cash, 7,000 ft. Wal't Lumber at $70.00 per M.

Cash Sales:—A. Comstock, 2 Pat. Rocker, $44.00 ; 2 Walnut Hat Rack, $55.00 ; Bunch of Cane, $1.60.

3,

Sold C. Gardiner, Brockville, 4 No. 42 Ash Beds, $36.00 ; 4 No. 42 Ash Dressers, $62.00 ; 2 No. 42 Ash W. Stands, $11.00, regular; and 4 No. 83 Ch., $6.16, net.

Sold W. Green, Wellington, 12 No. 6 Maple Ch., in the white, $21.60 ; 8 No 38 do., $9.60, net.

Sold Warner & Stone, Belleville, 12 Lounges, white, $15.00 ; 4 14 x 24 Glasses, $10.00, regular ; 48 No. 57 Ch., $27.00, net.

Cooper & Haight, Picton, repairing Bed and Bureau, $16.00 ; 2 Hair Soft Mattress, $9.00, regular.

Cash Sales :—H. LeBrun, 2 Ash Dining Table, and 12 No. 33 Ch., $52.00 ; 2 Wal't Washstand, $8.00.

4,

Sold H. Brennan, Ottawa, 48 No. 87 Ch., $26.00; 72 No. 89 Ch., Dark, $39.00 ; 24 No. 89, Light, $36.00, net.

Sold Geo. Lapum, Fairport, 8 Lounges, White, $10.00 ; 2 No. 42 Ash and Walnut Suite, $42.50, regular ; 4 No. 42 Ch., Light, $9.36, net.

R. Burns paid his note of $1,730.00, and interest at 6 per cent, due, to-day.

S. Jones pays his bill of Nov. 5th, $2,742.56, less discount 5 per cent on the regular portion of it.

Cash Sales :—2 Cong. Office chair, $36.00 ; 2 Office Desk, $90.

5,

Sold C. Gardiner, Brockville, 4 No. 48 Oak Ch., $5.20 ; 48 No. No. 89 Ch., $26.00 ; 2 Walnut Cor. Stand, $7.50, net.

Sold Warner & Stone, Belleville, 2 No. 33 Wal't Wood Top Suit, $72.00 ; 12 Com. S. B. Beds, $24.00, regular ; 4 No. 33 Wal't W. T Dressers, $68.00, net.

Sold W. Green, Wellington, 2 No. 33 Wal't W. T. Suit, $72.00 ; 2 No. 33 Wal't W. T. Washstand, $15.00, regular ; 48 No. 87 Ch., $26., net.

Cash Sales :—E. J. Clegg, 2 W. T. Suit, $72.00 ; 2 Ash Dining Table, $36.00.

Bought Damask, Jute, &c., of A. Ashton & Co., by check, $236.88; Invoice filed.

Deposited $5,000.

6,

Sold Lee Bros , Oxford, 4 No. 33 Wal't W. T. Suits, $139.00, regular ; 12 No. 59 Ch., $24.00, net.

H. Fraser, Picton, 2 No. 2 Couch in Carpet, $18.00; 12 Lounges, white, $25.80, regular ; 24 No. D. R. Ch., white, $8.70, net.

D. Pierson, Toronto, 4 No. 42 Ash Beds, $36.00 ; 4 No. 42 Ash

Dressers, $62.00; 2 No. 42 W. Stand, $11.00, reg.; 12 No. 83 Chairs, $18.00, net.

Cash Sales :—Parlor Suit, Waln't $144.00. Chamber Suit Walnut, $110.00.

Warner & Stone pay their net bill of Nov. 7 by check, $432.80.

The Foreman in the Cabinet Shop has handed in the time of, and amt. due to, the following hands; J. Dunlap, $21.00 ; C.Young, $23.50; L. Gillespie, $25.60 ; W. Hamilton, $13.00 ; S. Morton, $33.80; W. Case, $10.00 ; S. Toby, $16.60 ; J. Z. Rogers, $29.00 ; J. J. Long, $29.00 ; H. Stenson, $24.50 ; J. F. Jackson, foreman, $50.00. From the Warehouse are added C. C. Currie, book-keeper, $60.00 ; Wm. Moxon, ass't book-keeper, $16.00 ; I. K. Davis, salesman, $36.00 ; F. May, 40.00.

Note :—Credit the hands with their earnings in the Credit Column of the Hands Register weekly. Charge them with what they get when you pay them anything, by entering it in the debit column of H. R. Balances are carried forward weekly. You do not pay them anything this week.

8,

Sold Geo. Lapum, Fairport, 4 No. 33 Wal't W. T. Dressers, $68 ; 4 No. 33 Wal't W. T. W. Stands, $30.00, regular.

Cooper & Haight, Picton, 2 No. 35½ Ash Suit, $49.10 ; 2 No 50 Shelf Side Stand, $7.50, reg ; 8 No. 44 Ch., $7.34 ; 4 No. 27 Ch., $3.40 ; 24 No. 87 Ch., $13.00, net.

H. Brennan, Ottawa, 4 No. 33 Wal't W. T. Suits, $100.00, reg.; 20 Spindle H'd and F't Beds, $48.00, net.

Sent check on Ontario Bank to Stethem & Co., Peterborough, for bill of Hardware, $636.90.

Cash Sales :—2 Wal't M. T. Chamber Suits, $236.00 ; 2 Walnut Parlor Suits in Rep., $170.00.

Bought a new Planer, by check, $1,650.00.

9,

Sold S. Jones. Perth, 2 Book Cases, in white, $36.00, reg.; 72 No. 48 Oak Ch., $108.00, net.

Warner & Stone, Belleville, 48 No. 87 Ch., $26.00 ; 48 No. 89 Ch., $28.00 ; 24 No. 89 Ch. $13.50, net.

W. Green, Wellington, 2 No. 42 Ash and Wal't Suite, white, $42.50, reg ; 4 No. 80 Ch., $2.16 ; 24 No. 98 Ch., $64.00, net.

Cash Sales :—12 Dining Ch., $18.00 ; 2 Book Cases, Wal't, $90.

Gave check for 13,700 ft. Cherry Lumber, @ $48.00 per M.

Deposited $3,000.00.

J. K. Pierce pays his note of $1,900.00, with interest, in cash.

10,

Sold Lee Bros., Oxford, 12 Lounges, white, $15.00; 4 No. 1 Couches in Carpet, $35.00, reg : 12 No. 25 Ch., $14.40; 24 No. 57 Ch., $18.00, net.

C. Gardiner, Brockville, 4 No. 42 Ash Beds, $36.00; 4 No. 42 Ash Dressers, $62.00, regular; 8 No. 309 Ch., $80.00, net.

D. Pierson, Toronto. 6 14 x 24 Glasses, $16.50; 4 No. 33 Wal't W. T. Suites, $150.00; bunch Cane, $1.60, reg; 2 No. 309 Ch., $20. net.

Cash Sales :—2 Tete in Jute, $32.00 ; 2 Ford Rocker, $16.00 ; 2 Arm Chair, $12.00.

H. Brennan pays his reg. bill, $368.60, and his net bill of $390.20, of Nov. 10th, less discount 5 per cent on the reg. bill.

11,

Sold Cooper & Haight, Picton, 12 Ash and Wal't Beds, $72.00, reg ; 36 No. 57 C., in white, $31.00; 48 No. 25½ Ch., $60.00, net.

Geo. Lapum, Fairport, 24 No. 4 W.T. Cent, Tables, $84.00, reg ; 48 No. 59 Ch., $29.00, net.

H. Brennan, Ottawa, 4 No. 1 Book Cases, in white, $74.00; 4 No. 33 Ash and Wal't Suits, $137.00; 4 No. 98 Ch., $11.00, net.

Cash Sales :—2 W. T. Wash Stands, $9.00; 2 M. T. Suits, $112 ; 2 Office Desk, $68.00; 2 Office Chair, $30.00.

Deposited, $2.000.

12,

Sold S. Jones, Perth, 6 No. 42 Ash and Wal't Suits, $126.00; 16 S. W. Beds, $48.00, reg.; 8 No. 43 Light Ch., $9.00 ; 4 No. 25 dark Ch., $9.60, net.

W. Green, Wellington, 4 No. 33 Wal't Beds, $42.; 4 No. 33 W.T. Dressers, $68.00, reg.; 48 No. 72 Ch.; light, $22.00; 24 No. 72 Ch., dark, $11.00, net.

Cash Sales :—2 M. T. Wal't Side Boards, $96.00; 2 Wal't D. Table, $48.00; 18 D. Ch., $27.00.

13,

Sold H. Brennan, Ottawa, 4 M. T. Wal't Sideboards, $116.00 ; 4 Wal't D. Tables, $76.00, reg ; 36 No. 36 Ch., $48.00, net.

H. Fraser, Picton, 4 No. 33 Ash and Wal't Suites, $128.00; 4 No. 4 S. W. Beds, $16.00; 16 Com. Washstands, $24.00, reg; 24 No. 80 Ch., $24.00, net.

D. Pierson, Toronto, 4 No. 35 Ash Suites, $102.00; 4 Wal't D. Tables, $56.00, reg; 48 No. 44 Ch., $56.00, net.

Sales for Cash :—2 Couches in Carpet, $36.00; 2 Pat. Rocker, $44.00; 6 Office Stools, $7.20.

Lee Bros. pay their R. bill of Nov. 3, less discount, in cash

Deposit in Ontario Bank, $3,000.00.

Jackson, foreman, has left his time book in the office, from which the pay roll will be made up. The hands have earned, during the week, as follows :—Dunlap, $23.50; Young, $23.00; Gillespie, $28.40; Hamilton, $17.50; Morton, $31.00; Case, $13.50; Toby, $19.60; Rogers, $26.40; Long, $32.50 Stenson, $25.00; Jackson, foreman, $50.00. Added from the office and warehouse, Currie, book-keeper, $60.00; Moxon, assistant book-keeper, $16.00; Davis, salesman, $36; May, salesman, $40.00. Entered on Hands Register, and paid in full, in cash. Enter Cash also in C. B. " By Wages " total sum paid.

Inventories :

    Real Estate (Factory) $30,000.
    Warehouse $40,000.
    Mdse $23,729.80.
    Machinery & Tools $11,650.   Cash balance,
    Office Fixtures $700. $1,085.20
    Bal. Invty. (Interest) $25.13.

Accounts used in Ledger, with number of lines required for each, as follows :—

J. Campbell & Co., 3; Real Estate, 2; Cash, 2; Mdse., 10; Machinery & Tools, 3; Fixtures, 2; Bills Rec., 4; Interest, 4; Discount, 5; C. Gardner, 6; S. S. Jones, 5; Warner & Stone, 7; H. Brennan, 8; Ontario Bank, 7; Lee Bros., 5; Cooper & Haight, 7; W. Green, 9; D. Pierson, 9; H. Fraser, 8; G. Lapum, 9; Salary, 3; Loss and Gain, 6; Balance, 21.

REMARKS
— ON —
WHOLESALE GROCERY, SET 5.
BUSINESS PROSPEROUS—THREE PARTNERS.

The Invoice Book is used for pasting in the Bills of all purchases of Mdse. The total amount of the Invoices is posted at the end of each month to the Debit of Mdse.; and the persons from whom you bought should be credited daily. When the purchase is for cash mark it C. B. and post from the C. B.

The Sales Book is kept for entering all sales of Mdse., name of purchaser, amount, date, and mode of settlement. The total sales are posted at the end of each month to the credit of Mdse., and the purchaser should be debited daily, for the amount of his purchase. For the manner of making entries in this book see Manufacturing set 4. The S. B. here, however, need not have extra columns provided for reg. and net as the sales are made for various considerations, and may all be put in the same column.

Gains and losses for convenience may be divided in the following proportions. Student 7 ; Duncumb 6. Laing 7⅓.

This will give results nearly accurate.

Books used are Journal, Sales Book, Invoice Book, Cash Book, Bill Book and Ledger.

Trade discount should be closed into Mdse. account so as to get the true loss or gain on Mdse.

INVOICE BOOK.
OTTAWA, Wednesday, November 1st, 1889.

Nov.	1	To Bills Pay at 4 mos. per B.B. Invoice No. 1	605	88		
"	"	" Cash Kinlock & Lindsay. Inv. No. 2	658	38		
"	"	" Bills Pay Dominion Tea Co. Inv. No. 3	643	40		
"	2	" Bills Pay Kinlock & Lindsay. Inv. No. 4	757	80		
		Total to debit of Mdse (R.I.)....			2665	46

NOTE.—In actual business the above entries would represent the condensed statements on the invoices themselves. The invoices being folded up and pasted at the top to the book. There should be money columns ruled to the right, on the book itself. It is not necessary to mention the items because the Invoices contain full particulars. The student should continue I. B. as here commenced.

SET V,—WHOLESALE.

Ottawa, Ont., 1st November, 1889.

Student having previously conducted a Retail Grocery business, at a loss, determines to open a wholesale house for the purpose of making money, so he, C. Duncumb, and Walter Laing, have formed a copartnership for the purpose of conducting a Wholesale Grocery Business, under the firm name of Student, Duncumb & Co. Its gains and losses to be divided according to investment.

Student invests cash in Bank of Ottawa, $7,000—(C. B,) being the cash value of his resources resulting from Retail Set. plus $4,426.66.

C. Duncumb invests $6,000 cash which is deposited in Bank of Toronto. (J.)

Walter Laing invests as follows :—Cash per C. B., $2,590. Mdse per Statement, $4,500. James Stevenson's Note, Peterborough, Ont., at 3 mos. from August 15th, 1889. with interest at 7 per cent for $1,500. J. H. Secord owes him $350. Total $8,961.88 (C. B.-J. and B. B.)

Note :—The Interest on Stevenson's note must be reckoned and an account called "Interest Receivable," opened. This "interest receivable" has accumulated but is not due ; it goes to swell the investment and is placed among the resources. Calculate interest from August 15th to November 1st on $1,500 @ 7 per cent per annum.

Walter Laing owes as follows :—Note, favor of Arkell & Hutchinson, at 3 mos., from September 1st last, interest at 7 per cent. for $1,600. (J. and B. B.) Total $1,618.67.

Rented of J. P. Martyn, Store No. 15 Sparks Street, at an annual rental of $1200, to be paid monthly. (J. "Memo".)

Paid J. J. Blackmore & Co. for two office chairs @ $3.50 each ; 4 W. Chairs at $2.10 ; 1 Desk $20 ; ½ doz. Cane Chairs @ $12.00. (C. B. Debit "Fixtures" $41.40).

Paid James Ponsford for Office and Store Fixtures $280. (C. B. Debit "Fixtures").

Engaged Joseph Potts, as Book-keeper, @ $690 per annum, William Garland, W. H. Mountain and C. Bryson as Clerks, at $12.00 per week salary; and Fred Baldwin as Carrier, at $4.00 per week. (J."memo").

Bought of Redpath Sugar Refining Co., Montreal, on my acceptance at 4 mos., 25 bbls. R. Sugar @ 9c., 10 bbls. of 280 lbs., tare 210 lbs; 15 bbls. of 291 lbs. each, tare 223 lbs. (I. B.)

Received of J. H. Secord, check in full of ac. (C. B.) $350.

Bot. of Kinloch, Lindsay & Co., Montreal, for cash, 25 caddies "Myrtle Navy," 16½ lbs. each @ 35c.; 10 caddies " El Padre," 20 lbs. each @ 32c.; 15 boxes " Western Leaf," 1,500 lbs. @ 30c. Paid freight in cash, $7.75. (C. B.)

Discounted at Bank of Ottawa, Jas. Stevenson's note, dated August 15th last. Interest $26.25; Discount 17 days, $5.05. Proceeds placed to our credit. (C. B. & in B. B. write in " Remark Column " the words "Discounted Nov. 1st at B. of O.

Note :— Calculate the interest on this note to date of maturity ; add to principal, and find the discount on the sum for 17 days at 7 per cent per annum. Put your work down neatly on a slip of pa; *r* and place on file on teachers desk. Do this now.

Bot. of Dominion Tea Co., Toronto, Ont., on our acceptance at 4 mos., 10 chests C. Tea @ 50c., 75-11 lbs. each ; 12 chests Y. H. Tea @ 55c., 62-13 lbs. each. (I. B. and B. B).

2.

Sold Arkell & Hutchinson, for note at 3 mos., 5 chests Tea C @ 55c.

74-10, 72-11, 72-11, 79-14, 79-14; 14 bbls. Ref. Sugar @ 9¼ c., 280-19, 281-21, 285-17, 279-8, 288-17, 287-16, 286-22, 283-23, 295-27, 287-15, 283-20, 275-15, 276-14, 267-9; 5 caddies 16½ lbs. each, " Myrtle Navy" @ 45c.

Bot. of Kinloch, Lindsay & Co., for note at 4 mos., 12 sacks H. Coffee @ 31c., 132-9, 130-8, 135-10, 141-12, 145-12, 142-10, 143-10 ; 134-8, 147-13, 146-13, 148-13, 136-11 ; 10 bbls. Granulated Sugar @ 10½c., 281-21, 283-21, 284-29, 293-24, 290-23, 285-20, 286-19, 283-25, 290-22, 291-21.

3.

Bot. of H. Harmor & Sons, London, Ont., on a/c at 4 mos., 25 boxes V. Raisins, 28lbs., each @ 9⅛c.; 8 sacks of Rice @ 3¼ c., 192-3, 164-3, 173-3, 156-3, 163-3, 143-3, 153-3, 165-3.

Paid freight on same in cash $5.75.

4.

Sold James Best for his note at 3 months, 4 sacks Rice @ 4¼ c., 192-3, 164-3, 173-3, 156-3 ; 10 boxes V. Raisins 20 lbs. each @ 12c.; 5 bbls. Ref. Sugar @ 9¾c., 280-19, 281-21, 285-17, 279-8, 288-17.

6.

Sold Bannell Sawyer for cash, 3 sacks Sago, @ 5c., 134-3, 131-3, 136-3; 4 sacks R. Coffee @ 45c., 132-9, 130-8, 135-10, 141-12; 5 boxes P. Starch @ 7¼c., 37; 38, 35, 40, 41.

7.

Sold James Munn, city, for cash, 2 bbls. Syrup 40 gals. each @ 80c.; 5 bbls. Gran. Sugar @ 11¼c., 281-21, 283-21, 284-29, 293-24, 290-23; 10 lbs. Soda @ 6c.; 50 lbs. Currants @ 8½c.

8.

Bought of Redpath Sugar Refining Co., Montreal, for note at 4 months, 25 bbls. Ref. Sugar @ 9¼c., 270-20, 273-21 275-21, 280-24, 273-19, 285-22, 286-23, 284-22, 282-21, 284-23, 286-22, 287-23, 288-23, 289-24, 287-25, 281-19, 283-23, 297-25, 277-19, 273-20, 275-20, 268-19, 269-19 288-24, 280-10.

Paid Fred Baldwin a week's salary.

My private appropriations this week, cash $10, Groceries $15, C. Duncumb, $25 cash.

Sold Jas. Moore, on ac., 5 bbls. Granulated Sugar @ 12c. 291-21, 290-22, 283-25, 286 19, 285-20; 5 kegs D. Prunes 75lbs. each @ 10½c.; 1 bbl. Ex. Icing Sugar, 193-21 @ 13c.; 1 chest C. Tea 81-12, @ 57c.; 1 cask E. M. Vinegar 100 gals. @ 55c.

10.

Bot. of Kinloch, Lindsay & Co., Montreal, at 30 days, 50 boxes Corn Starch 60 lbs. each @ 7¼c.; 50 boxes Dried Herrings @ 23c.; 5 chests Gunpowder Tea @ $5.00 a chest; 10 boxes Cooks' Friend, 6 doz. each @ $2.35 per doz.; 40 boxes Ball Blue 25 lbs. each box @ 12½c. per pound.

11.

Sold Arkell & Hutchinson on 2 mos., 5 bags Java Coffee @ 35c., 506 lbs. net; 5 lbs. Cloves @ 45c.; 5 lbs. Nutmegs @ 50c.; 5 boxes Corn Starch 200 lbs. @ 12c.; 2 cases Ginger at $8.50; 2 boxes Red Herring at 25c.; 2 boxes Cooks' Friend, 4 doz. each, at $2.25; 20 gals. Erg. M. Vinegar at 45c.

12.

James Best, being unable to pay acceptance in full at maturity, asks us to accept his check for $82.38 and a sight draft on H. Harmor & Sons, London, Ont., for balance, agreed.

13.

Draw on W. Evans at 60 days sight to balance ac. with Kinloch, Lindsay & Co.

14.

Remitted H. Harmor & Sons, sight draft on Bank of Montreal to balance ac. Exchange ⅛ %. Discount off bill 5 per cent.
Note:—Add 25c. for collection.

15.

Received of Jas. Moore to apply on ac. $50.00.

16.

Bot. of Kinloch, Lindsay & Co. on 30 days, 80 cases Vinegar at $10.50. Paid freight in cash $6.75.

17.

Bot. of P. Innes & Co., Toronto, on note at 4 mos., 20 chests J. Tea at 65c., 81-12 each; 20 chests Y. H. Tea at 35c., 110-22 each; freight on same $15.24.

18.

Sold Bannell Sawyer on account, 10 chests O. Tea at 50c., 64-12, 62-14, 60-13, 58-12 57-10, 63-12, 64-12, 60-12, 61-14, 63-14; 10 boxes Starch 35 each at 6¼; 10 caddies M. N. Tobacco, 22, 21, 19, 20, 18½, 16, 19, 17, 22, 23, at 60c.

20.

Received Cash of Bannell Sawyer in full of ac.

23.

Remitted check on Bank of Ottawa to Kinlock, Lindsay & Co., to balance account. Discount allowed 3 p.c.

24.

Sold James Moore on note at 2 mos., 3 bbls. Refined Sugar, 290-22, 291-23, 293-22, at 9¼c.; 3 chests J. Tea, 61-13, 60-12, 58-12, at 57c.; 2 boxes Corn Starch, 40 lbs., at 15c.

25.

W. Evans has accepted draft. Date of acceptance, Nov. 24th.
Note :—No entry needed. It was anticipated in first entry that he would "accept."

27.

Sold Arkell & Hutchinson on ac., 20 boxes M. N. Tobacco, 19 lbs. each, at 70c.

Sold James Best for note at 3 mos., Mdse. per Invoice $750.36.

30.

Paid messenger a week's salary.

Drew on Arkell & Hutchinson at sight to balance ac. Had same discounted at Bank of Ottawa. Discount 7 per cent. per annum. Proceeds to our credit $55.

Discounted all notes in our possession.

Paid expenses for the month as follows:—Rent, $100; bookkeeper, $57.50; 3 clerks each $48; stationery, &c., $3.70.

Take off Balance Sheet, close Ledger and leave it ready to go on with next month's business, after which take off Trial Balance.

Inventories:—Fixtures, $200. Mdse $7,968.33.

Footings of Trial Balance, $32,702.92.

Accounts used in Ledger with number of lines required. C. Duncumb, 5; Student, 6; W. Laing, 6; J. H. Secord, 4; Kinlock, Lindsay & Co., 6; Interest and Discount 10; Bills Rec., 5; Mdse., 10; B. Pay., 4; Trade Discount, 6; Salary, 7; J. Moore, 5; Arkell & Hutchinson, 6; W. Evans, 4; Bannell Sawyer, 4; Bank of Ottawa, 5; Fixtures, 5; Expense, 7; Cash, 3; Exchange, 3; Loss and Gain, 12; Balance, 10.

REMARKS
— ON —
ADMINISTRATORS' SET, 6.

Books used:—Journal-Day-Book and Ledger.

The administrator is first to make a careful inventory of the Estate to be liquidated. His first work is to collect outstanding accounts and settle claims against the estate. The Canadian Statutes provide for his fee, or remuneration, allowing from 1 to 5 per cent. on the net value of estate. In cases where an estate is insolvent a fair allowance is generally made; and in the case of an estate of very considerable proportions, a fair lump sum is often allowed. An executor is a person appointed by the will to settle the affairs of the estate. His duties are similar to that of an administrator. An administrator's position is a very responsible one, and should not be entered upon without deliberation; bonds to the value of the estate are generally exacted of administrators, who are responsible to the full value of the estate for all that they do.

Open no Cash account; the cash received is invariably deposited in Merchants Bank, and checks are issued for all payments on the Bank.

ADMINISTRATORS' SET.
PETERBORO', JAN'Y 20, 1889.

1.—Student has been appointed Administrator of the Will of the late Richard King. The Will provides that the widow of the deceased, Ellen King, shall receive one-half of all the Estate, and that the four children, Thomas, Emma, John, and Norman, shall each receive $\frac{1}{4}$ of the remainder of said Estate.

The following is a schedule of the real and personal property pertaining to the Estate :

Farm property, $10,000; homestead, $3,000 ; machinery for farm work, $1,000; live stock, $2,500; village house and lot, $500, willed to Thomas ; Ontario Bank Stock, $10,000; deposit in Ontario Bank $500.00 ; and Merchants' Bank, $1,200.00 ; judgment against K. McCurdy, dated Jan. 2nd, 1888, $470.00; interest to date, 18 days @ 6% ; 12 Central Canada L. & S. Co's 6 per cent bonds, $500 each at par ; interest accrued on same from October 20, 3 months ; Wm. Argue's note at 6 months, dated August 1st, 1888, $375.00 ; interest accrued on same to date at 7 per cent ; James Langford's note at 2 mos. dated Dec. 15th, 1888, @ 12 per cent, $67.00 ; deposit in C. C. L. & S. Co., $750.00 ; interest accrued on same, from Jan. 1st, @ 5 per cent per annum. (J.)

2.—You wish to know to what extent the Estate is indebted and you publish for at least one calendar month the following notice in the County papers :

Note :—The Student will count the words in the following advertisement—each figure and initial letter when standing alone counts a word, each word in the heading counts two words. There are usually 8 words to a line; and the charge will be the usual rate of 8c. per line for the first and 2c per line for each subsequent insertion. To find the cost count 88 lines for 26 days at 8c. a line for first insertion, and 2c. a line for 25 insertions, then multiply by 2 as it is in two papers.

NOTICE TO CREDITORS
OF THE LATE RICHARD KING,
Late of the Township of Douro, County of Peterborough,
Farmer, deceased.

Pursuant to Section 34 of Chapter 107, of the Revised Statutes of Ontario, as amended by 46 Victoria, Chapter 9, Section 1, notice is hereby given, that the Creditors of the said late Richard King, who died on or about the 25th day of November, 1888, and any other persons having any claim against his Estate, are, on or before the 19th day of Jan'y, A. D., 1889, to send by post, prepaid, to *Student*, of the Town of Peterborough, in the County of Peterborough, Esquire, the Administrator of the Estate of the said deceased, their Christian and surnames, addresses and description, the full particulars of their claims, a statement of their accounts, and the nature of the securities (if any) held by them. And take notice that after the said 19th day of January next, the assets of the said deceased will be distributed among the parties entitled thereto, having regard only to the claims of which notice shall then have been received, and the said Administrator will not be liable for the assets so disposed of, or any part thereof, to persons whose claims shall not have been received by him by the said date.

STUDENT,
Administrator of the Estate of the late Richard King.
Dated Peterborough, Ont., Dec. 11th, 1889.

22.—In answer to your advertisement and efforts, you have ascertained that the deceased was indebted to the following persons for the sums named :—

James Fenton, for hay and straw, $75.00 : Robert Falls, for blacksmithing, $37.50 ; Atkinson & Co., store account, $123.75 ; D. Johnston, for carpentering, $13.25 ; John Drelin, labor, $7.85.

23.—Sold to-day by private sale :—50 sheep @ $3.25 per head, to John Fenton on his note at 3 months, with interest payable at Merchant's Bank ; one span carriage horses, (95 + 120) $215 00, to John McBride, on his note at 3 months, endorsed by Wm, McBride ; one yearling filly, $75.00, to Wm. Argue, for note at 2 months, with interest, endorsed by Thomas Argue ; to John Hodgins, 7 head cattle, $23.25. $32.00, $45.00, $38.00, $37.00, $28.50, $27.00, note @ 3 months, with interest ; poultry to James Allen for cash, $25.75 ; one set cart harness, $12.00, one set carriage harness, $50.00, and one lot of odd pieces, $13.50, to James Watt for his endorsed note @ 3 months, with interest.

24.—Paid Robert Falls, Atkinson & Co., D. Johnston, and John Drelin in full of account per check on Merchants' Bank.

25.—John Fenton pays his note to-day, deducting contra account. Interest to date.

27.—Sold by public auction, for cash, farm sundries, amounting to $750.00. Paid auctioneer $10.00 and 2 per cent of sales for his services.

28.—Disposed of the bonds to Mrs. Jas. Fenton, for cash, at par, with accrued interest. Deposit in Merchants' Bank.

29.—Rec'd payment in full for insurance on the life of the late R. King, $5,000.00. Policy was made in favor of wife.

NOTE.—No entry. This does not belong to Estate. She is not heir to it by Will. It is her own personal property, having been made in her favor.

30.—Discount the following notes at Merchants' Bank at 7 per cent:—John McBride, Wm. Argue, John Hodgins, Jas. Watt. (Discounted for the whole length of time for which notes were drawn.)

31.—Thomas King asks leave to occupy his house, situated in village. (Granted.) Heir by Will.

FEBRUARY 2.

Draw out amount, with accrued interest, from Central C. L. & S. Co., and deposit in Merchants' Bank.

3.—Pay John and Norman King $50.00 each.

4.—Norman King wishes to purchase the homestead, cattle and machinery now remaining, agreed, at appraised value.

9.—Paid Lawyers' expenses and other costs in connection with suit against K. McCurdy, $37.50.

10.—Rec'd through Solicitors, payment for judgment against K. McCurdy, a deed for Lot 26, N.E. corner George and London streets, appraised value, $350.00. Cash for balance.

Note:—(a) Posting should now be done, taking off a Trial Balance, and then close all loss and gain accounts directly into the R. King Estate account.

(b) Each subsequent entry should be posted as soon as journalized.

11.—Write out check in your own favor on Merchants' Bank, for Administrator's fee, as provided by law. Do not count the expenses or liabilities. (b) Appropriate your fee per check on Merchants' Bank @ 3 p. c.

Note:—Canadian law allows as high as 5 p. c. to the administrator, generally, according to the degree of difficulty in "winding up" the estate.

12.—Divide up the net credit of the estate as best you can, so that each heir may receive his share in full. Nelson is to have the homestead and the widow to have the farm property.

Accounts should now balance.

Accounts used, with number of lines occupied by each, as follows:—King Estate, 8; Real Estate, 7; Machinery, 7; Live Stock, 10; Ontario Bank Stock, 5; Merchants' Bank, 20; K. McCurdy, 4; C. C. L. & S. Co. Bonds, 4; C. C. L. & S. Co. 4; J. Fenton, 4;

Robert Falls, 4 ; Bills Receivable, 11 ; Atkinson & Co., 4 ; D. Johnson, 4 ; J. Dreelin, 4 ; Expense, 6 ; Mrs. King, Thomas, John and Emma, 4 each ; Norman King, 6 ; Interest and Discount, 12 ; Cash, 10.
Net Credit of Estate before Administrator's fee is deducted $
Footings of Trial Balance $41,199.53.

REMARKS
— ON —
SINGLE ENTRY, SET 7.

SINGLE PROPRIETORSHIP—BUSINESS PROSPEROUS.

FEATURES.

By this method accounts are kept with persons only.

All Resources and Liabilities that can be found by taking an Inventory are omitted from the books.

Cash receipts and payments are entered in the Cash Book ; B Rec. and B. Pay. in the Bill Book.

Invoice, Sales and Order Books are sometimes used.

To find the Net Gain or Loss, subtract the resources and liabilities and compare the result with the Net Investment.

All *transactions* are *posted direct* to the Ledger.

CHANGING FROM SINGLE TO DOUBLE ENTRY.

In changing from Single to Double Entry, first find the Resources and Liabilities ; the difference will be the Capital ; now credit Stock or the partners.

No changes should be made in accounts already opened in the Ledger, simply debit Resources and credit Liabilities, and open accounts with that species of property with which you wish to deal separately.

The Ledger should now be in balance—take off a Trial Balance.

SINGLE ENTRY.
Ottawa, Jan. 1, 1890.

Net investment of the proprietor at starting is $4,750, of which his Mdse is valued at $2,000, and cash makes up the balance.

J. D. Wallis, 2 Cr.
    By Mdse, as per. Invoice.....................$ 800

W. H. Thiles,   Dr.
    To one case Gray Sheeting, 1,200 yds. @ 25c......

J. P. Anderson, Jr.,   3   Dr.
    To Mdse, as per bill..........................$ 150

J. K. Stewart,   5   Dr.
    To 8 pcs. Cassimere, 320 yds. @ $1.50..........
    " 25 yds. Sheeting @ 30c.....................
    " 40 " Gray Cotton @ 12c...................
    " 18 " Silk Velvet @ $4.00................

W. J. Stephens,   6   Dr.
    To Mdse., as per bill.........................$ 500

Chas. Stewart,   8   Dr.
    To Mdse., as per bill......... ....$1.200

A. Johns,   9   Dr.
    To Mdse., as per bill.........................$1.500

Contra.
    By note @ 90 days for........................$1.200

Allan Grant   12   Dr.
    To Mdse., as per bill.........................$ 450

W. J. Stephens,   Cr.
    By cash on account..........................$ 200
    " draft @ 30 days on C. Claghorn for...........$ 150

J. D. Wallis,   13   Dr.
    To cash on account..........................$ 800

Chas. Stewart   16   Cr.
    By cash on account ....$ 300

W. J. Stephens,   19   Cr.
    By cash in full of account.....................$ 150

J. P. Anderson, Jr.,   Cr.
    By draft @ 30 days in full of account............$ 150

Inventory.
    Mdse., per Stock Book.......................$ 750

NOTE :—Having worked by Single Entry, next change to Double Entry and take of a Trial Balance.

FORM OF SINGLE

CASH.

1889.	Dr.			D. B.		
Aug.	2	To	Amount in Bank............................	1	1500	
"	"	"	" Till.....	1	100	
"	3	"	Proceeds of Shaver Draft.....................	1	130	09
"	"	"	" Vollett & Co Draft..............	2	19	75
"	5	"	Difference in Engines..........	2	250	
"	"	"	Clindinning & Co. per chk	3	40	
"	"	"	Raised on Std. Bk. note.....................	3	2938	35
"	"	"	Proceeds of Drafts as per D. B...............	4	116	79
"	"	"	" Faill Draft.......................	4	163	53
"	6	"	Cotton Co. to bal. acc......................	5	2	72
"	"	"	Difference in saws..........................	5	2	
"	"	"	Raised on Std Bk. Note........	5	994	40
"	"	"	One Steam Whistle....	5	3	68
"	"	"	Proceeds of Dom Fertilizer Works Draft.......	6	39	50
"	7	"	O. Peckham................................	7	25	
"	"	"	One ball Wick Packing.......................	7		15
"	8	"	Raised on Std. Bk. Note	9	498	03
"	"	"	One Small Pulley........	9		50
"	"	"	Proceeds of Herr & Co's Draft................	10	1141	67
					7966	16
"	"	"	Balance............		2782	

ENTRY CASH-BOOK.

CASH.

1889.					Cr.	
Aug.	3	By Stamps...	1	2	
"	5	" Freight on Planer and Matcher.................	3	5	
"	"	" Duty on Rubber Belting.....................	3	6	
"	"	" Standard Bank Note per chk..................	3	3000	
"	"	" Vollett & Co. Draft returned.................	4	20	
"	6	" Freight on Machinery and Belting............	5	3	06
"	"	" Standard Bank Note per chk..................	5	1000	
"	"	" Stamps.......................................	6	2	
"	7	" A. R. Cook's Private acc.....................	7	9	
"	"	" Stamps.......................................	7		75
"	"	" Exp. on goods from Tor. per chk............	7		40
"	"	" Shaver Draft returned dishonored............	8	130	34
"	8	" Std. Bk. Note $1,000 less dis. $5.24.........	8	994	76
"	"	" E. & F. Schmidlin...........................	8	7	65
"	"	" Stamps.......................................	9	1	
"	"	" Exp Paris and Return........................	9	1	25
"	"	" Balance (Red Ink)...........................		2782	95
				7966	16

REMARKS
— ON —
JOINT STOCK COMPANY'S, SET 8.

THE JOURNAL.

In Joint Stock Book-keeping the Journal is kept much the same as in ordinary business but there are some differences which we wish to explain.

The first entry made in a set of Joint Stock books is to credit capital and to debit the original subscribers for stock. We credit capital stock with the total amount of subscribed stock, and debit each share holder with the amount of his subscription. This is called the nominal capital of the company, and whenever a call is made cash is debited and subscriber is credited. When all the calls are paid the company then has a real capital amounting to the sum at the credit of the capital stock. If at any time it is desired to know the real capital of a company before all the capital is paid up, all that has to be done is to subtract the several sums at the debit of the shareholders from the total at the credit of the capital stock. When payments of stock are made credit the shareholders in the General Ledger and at the same time credit the subscribers in the Stock Ledger. Some Accountants credit the capital account as the sums are paid in by subscribers. Agents of the company who do business in the name and for the company are treated as *personal accounts* in ordinary business and the *results*, and not the details of their business, are entered in the books of the company at the head office. They are debited for all they receive and are credited for all they hand in to the company as per their own statements which must be abstracts of their own books. Then their accounts in the company's books should close.

When partially paid up stock is transferred, the entry is made in the Journal and an explanation in the Transfer Book. If the stock is fully paid up no Journal entry is made because the transaction does not effect the General Ledger. After the last entries for the year, half year or quarter, have been made the transactions are posted and a trial balance taken off. The accounts showing losses and gains should next be closed. As soon as you find the net result of the business you let the company know it through the Directors at their first meeting.

When cash account is closed bring down the balances, these show the resources and liabilities of the company. When this is done the statements of assets and liabilities and of losses and gains are made out. After being examined and reported on by a properly appointed Auditor, these statements are usually printed and circulated among the shareholders.

THE CASH BOOK.

This book is not unlike the Cash Book to be found in any well regulated office where the books are kept by double entry.

THE GENERAL LEDGER.

The first accounts in this book are the names of the original stock holders and the capital stock. Capital stock is always opened with a credit balance, and is not effected by anything except the reduction or increase of capital. When the stock is fully paid up then the shareholders accounts are closed up. Sometimes the Ledger is closed up before the capital is fully paid up, in this case the accounts of shareholders are closed "By Balance" thus showing a debit to the company like the other personal accounts.

THE STOCK LEDGER.

This book is one in which to keep an account of each stockholder whose interest in the company may at any moment be severed simply by transferring of stock. It is quite different in ordinary business where each partner must stay according to the terms of their agreement. For those who obtain paid up stock we open an account only in the Stock Ledger. But for those who receive stock not fully paid up we open an account both in the General and Stock Ledgers. And for this reason he at once becomes a debtor to the company for the amount of stock still unpaid and, when he transfers his stock if it is still unpaid, we debit the transferee both in the General and the Stock Ledger and for the same reason as we debit original subscribers. By reference to the Stock Ledger it will be seen that it contains the name and address of each shareholder, the number of shares he holds and the amounts paid by each. These items are brought from the C. B. as received. If all the claims have not been issued or have not been paid, the sum of the credits of this Ledger plus the sum to the debit of stockholders in the General Ledger, will just equal the sum at the credit of capital stock account in the G.L. After all the "calls" have been issued and paid the sum of the credits of this Ledger will just equal the sum at the credit of the capital stock account in the G. L.

Where the stock is soon to be called up or is to be fully paid up as subscribed for, there is no necessity for opening the accounts with subscribers in the G. L.

The books and forms commonly used in Joint Stock Company Book-keeping are as follows :

Asset and Liability Statement,   Minute Book,
By-laws (for reference),   Prospectus (for reference),
Cash Book,   Profit and Loss Statement,
Dividend Sheet,   Stock Ledger,
General Ledger,   Stock Certificate,
Instalment } Lists,   Trial Balance,
{ Scrip,   Transfer Book.
Journal,

REMARKS
— ON —
BANKING AND BANK BOOK-KEEPING, SET 9.

OPENING OF A BANK.

1. When a bank begins business, the General Book-keeper debits cash and credits capital. The Cash is transferred to the Paying Teller and the corresponding entries are then found in the General Ledger and in the Paying Teller's proof. The entire check list of the Bank continues to be credited daily to the Paying Teller, and all receipts including those from the Clearing House charged to him. It follows that the Teller's daily proof, if correct, must agree with the balance of the Cash account on the Ledger.

2. A separate account is kept of the different denominations of Circulating Bills which are issued by the Bank; also of the securities pledged with the Bank department in their redemption.

3. The General Book-keeper posts daily the Liquidations and the costs of Bills discounted to that account and the balance shows what

the addition of the Ticklers should be and precisely what amount of Bills Receivable should be on hand. The certification account shows the balance of outstanding certified checks.

4. He posts to expense a/c all salaries, rents and expenditures; likewise the debits and credits to interest, exchange and other a/cs. of this class. These are finally absorbed in Loss or Gain account when the books are made up for a dividend.

5. He keeps all a/cs. with foreign bankers, charging them with notes sent for collection and crediting remittances; and renders to them a monthly a/c current, or receives one as the case may be.

6. From the footings and balance of these various accounts is composed the "Bank Statement."

7. The General Book-keeper mostly has the Stock Ledger and Transfer Books in his custody.

From time to time the ledger is proved by making out a list of the Stockholders with the number of shares held by each which are entered by their par value and give the exact capital of the Bank. This is done necessarily 3 times a year——twice to ascertain who is entitled to receive a dividend, and once to know who has a vote for directors. The transfer books are closed for a short time previous to the payment of dividends so as to prevent wrong payments by an inaccurate list.

COMPARISON BETWEEN BANKING AND MERCHANTILE BOOK-KEEPING.

1. Merchants have Wastebook, Journal, Ledger. Bankers have Wastebook, Day Book, Ledger.

In both cases the Wastebook is the book in which transactions are first entered. But the book is capable of sub-division. It contains a record of various transactions, some of which may be entered in separate books. Bankers have their received, paid, and supplimentary wastebooks, also their " Deposit Receipt Books, " Discount Register and other books subsidiary to the Wastebook. So merchants have their Wastebook sub-divided into various books according to the nature of the transaction. There is the Invoice Book, containing an a/c. of all goods purchased; the Sales Book, containing an a/c. of all goods sold; a book for Bills Receivable, containing an account of all bills in the Merchants hands for which, when due, he will receive payment; another for Bills Payable containing a list of all bills he has accepted, and which when due, he will have to pay; a Cash Book containing an account of all cash he receives or pays away ; and several others, varying according to the character and extent of the business.

Now, all these sub-divisions of the Merchants Wastebook resemble those of the Bankers in two things—first, they are all kept chronologically—they contain a record of the transactions in the order of time in which they occurred; and secondly all the transactions thus recorded must afterwards, upon the system of Double entry, pass either individually or in totals through the book which Merchants call a Journal, and Bankers call a Day Book.

2. The words Journal and Day Book have the same meaning; and in this instance the use of the two books are similar, but in the merchant's Journal individual transactions may be entered, while in the Bank's Day Book they are always entered in totals. Thus the total amount of Bills Discounted and the total amounts of credits and payments on current accounts, are entered in the Day Book but not the individual items.

Another advantage is that over each entry in the Merchant's Journal you state to what account it is to be posted ; for every entry is posted in two accounts—to the debit of one account and to the credit of the other. And this is denoted as follows :

—— Mdse. Dr.
To Cash Cr——

Implying that the account Merchandise is to to be debited and the account Cash to be credited.

The entries in the Banker's Bay Book are made daily but the entries in the Merchant's Journal are generally made once a week or month.

3. We have stated that in the Merchant's Ledger every entry is made twice—one account being debited and another credited—and these two accounts are indicated 'n the Journal. Banks which have General Ledger keep their books by double entry. The "Current Accounts Ledger" is not kept by double entry. It contains nothing but personal accounts and its accuracy is tested only by the periodical balancings. The Bankers' Ledger that corresponds with the Merchant's Ledger is not the Current Accounts Ledger but the General Ledger for this only is kept by double entry.

The sum of all the debits should equal all the credits. But as the transactions in the Banker's General Ledger are not posted individually but only in totals the double entry does not appear on the face of the accounts. Thus if a bill be discounted for a customer and the amount placed to the credit of his current account, the Journal Entry, on the principle of mercantile book-keeping would stand thus :—

——Bills Discounted Dr.
To Current Accounts Cr.——

But the bill discounted is placed to the debit of the account of Bills Discounted being the title of all bills discounted on that day. And the amount is placed to the credit of Current Accounts on that day. Thus the double entry though equally real is not so apparent as though the transactions were posted individually.

4. The accounts in a merchant's ledger are easily classified into personal accounts, real accounts, and loss and gain accounts. The Banker's general ledger has no personal accounts, as these are all kept in the Current Accounts Ledger.

The usual accounts are as follows and are all either Real or Loss and Gain accounts.

CLASSES.
1. LODGEMENTS—balance always on the credit side.
2. INVESTMENTS—balance always on the debit side.
3. EXPENDITURES—
4. CASH-accounts with branches.
5. PROPRIETORS' accounts.

1 City Accounts Current—Country Accounts—Deposit Receipts—City Bills Deposited—Country Bills Deposited. Notes in circulation—Credits on Agents.

2 Bills Discounted—Country Bills Discounted—Past Due Bills—Government Stock—Bonds—Exchequer Bills—Loans to Customers—Loans to Brokers—Interest Accounts.

3. Bank Premises—Rent—Taxes—Salaries—Stationery—Incidental Expenses—Law Expenses.

4. Branch A—Branch B—Branch C.

5. Paid up Capital—Preliminary Expenses—Dividend Acccunts—Unclaimed Dividends—Surplus Fund—Loss and Gain Account—Fund for Bad Debts—General Account for Cash.

It would be quite possible (though not advisable) to introduce into the General Ledger all the Personal Accounts. And thus form the Current Account Ledger and the General Ledger into one book, which would make the whole thing double entry.

HINTS TO BANK CLERKS.

1. Good writing and figure-making necessary.
2. Quick "calling" of sums.
3. Quick counting.
4. Quick entering—holding and turning checks with left hand while writing with the other.
5. Quick adding and subtracting.
6. The principle of balancing pervades the whole system of bookkeeping.
7. Next to a knowledge of the names and functions of the different books, the terms and phraseology used must be thoroughly learned.
8. Books are sometimes named differently in different banks, and different terms employed to describe the same operations.
9. Everyone opening an account with the bank enters his name in a book called the "Signature Book" and the book is referred to if ever a draft is presented having a doubtful signature. The person is supplied free of charge with the papers, books, etc.
10. A check is cancelled by drawing a line through the signature.
11. CASH DEPARTMENT. Two waste books—Received Waste book and the Paid Waste book. In the former is entered an account of the cash received and in the latter is entered an account of all the checks and bills paid.
12. Checks on your own bank are to be entered by the name of the Drawer and the Amount.
13. The total of the "Received Wastebook" should be equal to the total of the Daybook.
14. Books used in this department: Wastebook Received and Paid; Money Book; Cash Book; Day Book; Current Account Ledger; Deposit Receipt Book.
15. BILL DEPARTMENT.

(*a*) There are two classes of bills namely, "Bills Deposited" and "Bills Discounted." The books used for these are respectively Bills Register and Discount Register.

(*b*) Bills Ledger and Discount Ledger. In these books a separate account is opened for each party.

(*c*) Bill Journals, Discount Journal. In these Journals the bills are entered under the respective days on which they fall due.

For this purpose the day of the week and the month are kept at the head of the page.

(*d*) Lists and Unpaid Lists are also kept.

16. CURRENT ACCOUNT.—When a sum is received to the credit of a current account it is entered in the "Received Wastebook," copied from thence into the Daybook and from thence into the Current Account Ledger.

When a check is paid to the debit of a current account it is entered from the check itself into the Paid Wastebook and the Current Account ledger,

17. BILL DISCOUNTED —When a bill is discounted the discount is calculated by the Accountant. If the party for whom it is discounted has a current account the full amount of the bill is placed to his credit and he is debited for the interest. If he have no account he is paid the amount.

In addition to the books used by Joint Stock Companies, the following books are used in Banks :

Collections { Register, Deposit Ledger,
{ Tickler, Foreign Draft Register,
Discounts { Register, General Ledger,
{ Tickler, Journal.

These books are often called by other names, but their uses are identical, or nearly so.

SOCIETY BOOK-KEEPING.

Society book-keeping is usually a slip-shod affair. Many Secretary treasurer knowing little or nothing about book-keeping, yet undertaking the management of society accounts that are often " considerable."

The first thing to do on taking charge of such books is to ascertain the resources and liabilities whenever they can be found ; next make a statement of them. By subtracting the sum of the one from the sum of the other the net worth or insolvency of the Society is found. Keeping in mind Societies in general, and Church Societies in particular, we can make room but for a few remarks.

To put accounts into good shape, the following books should be used, Cash Book, Journal, Pew Rent, Receipt Book, with stubs, Ledger and an auxiliary (Pew Rent) Ledger, and a "Dues" Ledger is sometimes used.

As pew rents are usually collected every 3, 6, or 12 months, the journalizing should be done at those times of each year as follows :—

Pew Holders, Dr.
To Pew Rent.

Then following this should be given the names, number of pew, and amount of rent due by each pew holder. In the General Ledger the total amount of all pew-holders indebtedness would be charged to an a/c. called "Pew-holders," and an account called "Pew Rents" would be credited.

The cash book should have, at least, one extra column on each side—the extra column on the debit side for "Pew-holders," another special column might be kept for "collections." Special columns on the credit side may be used for any "disbursements" of frequent occurrence.

The Auxiliary or Pew holders' Ledger is kept for Pew holders' accounts, only. When a man's pew rent becomes due he is charged in this Ledger; when he pays in part or in full he is credited with the amount.

All entries must be made in the Journal and Cash Book, posting is done direct from them to the General and to the Auxiliary Ledger. Two columns to the left of the entries in both J. and C.B. should be provided for, placing in one of them a page of the Aux. Ledger and in the page of the General Ledger while posting.

For all monies received, a receipt should in every in case be given and the particulars entered on the stub.

For all monies paid out receipts should in every case be taken and then numbered so as to correspond readily in the auditor's work, to the entries in the C.B.

The only special or peculiar Ledger titles in account-keeping of this kind would be "Society Account—corresponding to stock or proprietors ac. "Working Account" corresponding to Loss and Gain ac.

A statement at the close of the year should be laid before the Society showing the trial balance, receipts and discounts for the year, and the present assets and liabilities.

INDEX.

	PAGE
Administrator's Set, Remarks on	128
" Transactions,	129-31
Bookkeeping, Explanatory Notes and Illustrations	18-23
Books	24-31
Bill-book	27
Books as Evidence in Court	30
Bad Debts Account—How to write off	30
Balance Sheet	75
Branch Houses, Accounts with	30
Books Used in Retail Set	99
Banking & Bank Bookkeeping, Remarks on	138-143
Commission Sales Ledger	29
Cash Book	25
Continued Trial Balance	110
Cash Book, Samples of	84-104
Commission Sales Ledger, Sample of	104-105
Cash Journal, Remarks on	111
Cash Methods, Remarks on	111
Collateral Receipt Book (Sample of)	113
Collateral Security Register, Sample of)	116-117
Commercial Abbreviations	3-4
Day Book & Journal	24
Day Book Entries Journalized	33-35
Discounting and Renewing Notes and Drafts	53
Day Book Transactions to be Journalized	55-60
Detecting Errors in Trial Balance	65 and 70
Exhibiting Settlements in the Ledger	31
Exercises in Posting	70-79
Home Work	5-16
Hints to Bank Clerks	142
Invoice Book, Sample of	123
Journal Day Book	27
Journal Day Book, Sample of	84
Junior Practice, Directions for	85-87
Journal, Sample of	98
Joint Stock Cos. Bookkeeping, Remarks on ; Books	130-138
Joint Stock Co., Notes on	51
Ledger	20
Ledger, Transferring from Old to New	31
Letters, Samples of	87-94
Model Day Book	61
Model Journal	62
Model Ledger	63-64
Manufacturing, Remarks on	112-113
" Set Transactions	117-122
Names of Books Used in Joint Stock Cos.	138
Notes on Drafts	40
Order Book	97
Preface	3

INDEX.—CONTINUED.

	PAGE.
Personal Ledger	29
Private Ledger	29
Plant Account	31
Promissory Notes, Hints	36–38
Partnership Business	46–47
Personal Accounts Rec. and Payable	74
Personal Ledger, Sample of	96
Piece Work Time Book, Sample of	116
Pay Roll	116
Preface	8
Questions on Work covered by First Examination	23
" " " Second "	31–32
" " " Drafts Examination	79
" " Retail Set and Retail Examinations	102
Rules for Journalizing	18–21
Retail Set, Notes on	95
Remarks on Drafts	40–42
Results	65
Sales Book	26
Special Account Books	29
Special Column Journal	29
Shipments and Consignments, Notes on	43
Statements of Losses and Gains	64–81
Special Column Journal, Sample of	118
Set 1, 2, 3, Junior Practice	85-86-87
Shipment and Consignment Question	110
Statement of Resources & Liabilities	81
Set 3—Primary	82–83
Set 2 "	80
Shipments & Consignments	104
Sales Book, Sample of	115
Single Entry Remarks	132
" " Transactions	133
" " Cash Book	134–135
Society Bookkeeping	143–4
To the Student	18
Transferring Accounts from One Ledger to Another	81
Transactions in Cash	33
" with Bank	34
" on Account	35
" with Notes	38
" in Part Payment	39
" in Drafts	42
" in Shipments & Consignments	43–44
" in Partnership Settlements	47–50
" with Joint Stock Companies	51–53
" in Retail Set	99–102
" in Commission	105–110
Trial Balance	64, 66–73
Title	1
Weekly Time Book	114
Wholesale Grocery, Remarks on	123
What a Balance Sheet Should Show	74
Working Rules	85
Wholesale Transactions	124–126

www.ingramcontent.com/pod-product-compliance
Lightning Source LLC
Chambersburg PA
CBHW030346170426
43202CB00010B/1259